deviance
Crime and Behavior

M. HOLMES

isbn: 978-1-4907-9311-5 (sc)
isbn: 978-1-4907-9312-2 (e)

Library of Congress Control Number: 2019931100

 www.trafford.com

North America & international
toll-free: 1 888 232 4444 (USA & Canada)
fax: 812 355 4082

Deviance

CRIME AND BEHAVIOR

The Scholarly Writings of
M. Holmes

DEDICATION

"**Crime and Behavior**" is dedicated to many individuals who have touched my life in one way or another, especially my son, JL, deceased. I give thanks to God for all that He has done for me. God has shown me the way to successfully publish these writings in which I can share with the world. These writings are meant to inspire and enlighten people of all age groups as well as all nationalities. I am most proud to share these writings in which I wrote while in college at the young age of 65. It took courage for me to go back to school at that age. The reason I chose that path was - I wanted to make a difference. I would like to thank all of my professors who inspired me and pushed me to pursue my degree in criminal justice. These writings are a result of life experiences combined with what I have learned through being educated at the University and my life experiences. I am sharing with you a very intricate part of who I am. I hope that you understand and appreciate the content of these writings. Take what you need from them and attempt to make changes where you are able to do so and always remember "Change what you can and accept what you cannot change".

In addition to the above, always remember that crime has many faces. As we go forward it will become obvious to what I am communicating. What we understand crime to be is against the laws of society which is punishable by law. Unfortunately, crime has many faces. If we probe a little deeper some crimes are not always punishable by law. Some crimes go unpunished by law but are punishable in the eyes of God. Stay tuned.

CONTENTS

MY PURPOSE:

Once we know what God's purpose is for our lives, we must take the necessary steps to carry out God's purpose. My purpose is to utilize my gift of writing to help others. Sometimes we don't find out that purpose until late in life. I have known for some time now that I enjoy writing. What I didn't know - this was my purpose and passion. Now, I seem to be making up for lost time. I have had several jobs and most of the time they involved some type of writing. God, has also gifted me with great observational skills. Being observant is a key component in writing. I have taken many paths but they only lead me back to writing. I have learned many things along the way. Most importantly, it is those things that I have learned along the way I wish to share with you in this book. We must all learn to be patient and listen to our innermost thoughts while we are enhancing our gifts. Be careful not to allow yourself to give away that gift without compensation. Reason being, it then becomes exploitation. Once you allow exploitation to take root you will definitely become hostile. If, hostility takes root you might find yourself on the wrong path and that path may lead to crime or incarceration. This is not something that you want associated with your God given Gifts.

Moreover, it is when we become impatient we take the wrong paths. Once you become aware of your purpose ("Gift") then you begin to take steps to enhance that gift. It takes education, get the education. Remember patience is the key component here. The problems with our youth today is the lack of patience. Patience is a learned behavior. We learn this through our home environment. In families that are economically deprived it is much more difficult to focus on your purpose, but we must strive for purpose and perseverance.

We just experienced our 2016 Presidential Election and now the nation is divided. We must be vigilance in how we respond to the climate of these United States. We must not fall prey to the negativity of the climate. We must strive to overcome the hand in which society has dealt us. As you go forward in reading this book, I hope that you keep things in perspective. Read, learn and stay positive. This book is met to help all that read and digest its contents and to help and direct our paths. Most importantly, to help guide our youth today and any future youth. We could only accomplish this if we share the contents of this book.

INTRODUCTION

Three years ago I decided to return to college to get my Bachelor Degree in Criminal Justice. I decided on criminal justice because I was frustrated with the number of youths going to prison. The only way that I knew to combat the problem was to learn about our criminal justice system and to create theories and solutions in which to stop the crimes. Most importantly, to stop the revolving doors to our prisons. At times, I became so angry and frustrated because of the crimes in society. There are reasons for the crimes and I believe that we are not doing enough to halt the crimes. I have determined that the reasons for the crimes in our society are not unfounded. We need to take our heads out of the sand and address the issues. I believe that the issues are basically economics. Our society runs on economics. Just, what is economics? The Oxford Dictionary defines economics as "the science concerned with the production and consumption or use of goods and services." In order to live a healthy and prosperous life we must be economically fit. In society today, we have many families and individuals who are economically deprived, resulting in crime. This I believe is the root of all the crime in our society. The lack of a good life. In order to rectify the situation we must get to the root of society's problems. What makes people commit crimes? When do people commit crimes? Where do people commit crimes? If we stop to answer these questions perhaps we can begin to slow crime down. There are so many reasons for the crime. People are frustrated with their lives and attempt to make wrong decisions. Decisions which are against society's laws. Life is not easy. We all are entitled to a good foundation and that foundation begins at home. The scholarly writings of M. Holmes will attempt to cover different topics which is pertinent to the understanding of society today. This book reveals the theories of the author and her solutions on cleaning up the mess. If curiosity is the reason you selected this book to read let it serve as the beginning to an end to the crime in society today. We as decent human beings should not look back but forward to a better society. And, to do this we must begin to rebuild. As you read this book remember to constantly think about what you can do to prevent crime. In this book there will be various true events to help you to realize the significance of the situation. We often overlook what is happening in our everyday lives without realizing how we might contribute to the problems of today. Think about the children – they are our future.

To begin, let us examine our integrity. Integrity is the foundation of all our actions. What does the Bible say about integrity? "Integrity is the quality or state of being of sound moral principle: uprightness, honesty, and sincerity". Proverbs 2:20-21 says it all. "So you will walk in the way of the good and keep to the paths of the righteous. For the upright will inhabit the land, and those with integrity will remain in it…" If we are to begin to make changes in society we all should be honest with ourselves. In our society today we are divided. We have those who believe that they are better than others, which brings on a negative mindset. Take a journey back in history for the moment. When Africa was invaded by Europeans they attempted to exploit Africa through imperialism. This worked for a while until some became enlightened to what was taking place in Africa. Without giving you a complete history lesson, I want to bring your focus back to the present right here in these United States. In many instances, we have the same problems but among the races. There are some people who believe that they are better than others and want to always maintain that status quo. As a result, we have people in our society making decisions to acquire their piece of the pie, but are making the wrong decisions. Our problems in society will not go away overnight, however we can begin now to rectify the situation. We must stop the exploitation of human beings in society and maintain our integrity as it is meant to be. We must give the underprivileged a fair chance of a good lifestyle. How we do this, is through equal opportunities.

In today's society this is not always the case. In many businesses racism is alive and well. It is the individuals who own the businesses, direct the businesses and who set the tone of the businesses. It all comes down from the top. I have firsthand knowledge of experiencing racism. And, from racism comes exploitation. Furthermore, if you allow another to exploit your God given gifts then you allow the economic balance to shift. As I mentioned earlier, I will give short anecdotes of real individuals that will make you aware of the truths behind my theories. This book is met for individuals who would like to see positive changes in our society. I cannot stress enough, we need to save our children.

For the Lord said, "I will instruct thee and
teach thee in the way which thou shall
go; I will guide thee with mine eye."

Challenge yourself, make changes where changes can be made. Remember, "change the things that you can; and accept what you cannot change." There are chapters in this book where you can make resolutions or comments. Feel free to make the notation that will change things in a positive way.

SECTION I

CRIME AND ITS EFFECT ON HUMANITY

CHAPTER ONE

HATE CRIMES

This paper will be based on "Hate Crimes", which means "A criminal offense in which the motive is hatred, bias, or prejudice based on the actual or perceived race, color, religion, national origin, ethnicity, gender, or sexual orientation of another individual or group of individuals." I will attempt to describe how the crime is measured according to the Uniform Crime Report (UCR). The UCR is defined "as official data on crime in the United States, published by the Federal Bureau of Investigation (FBI). UCR is a nationwide, cooperative statistical effort of nearly 18,000 city, university and college, county, state, tribal, and federal law enforcement agencies voluntarily reporting data on crimes brought to their attention." The UCR gathers data on who typically commits the crime, who is typically the victim of the hate crime, where this type of crime is mostly to be committed, it describes the trend for the hate crimes and explain what is done as far as reporting hate crimes.

First, I would like to begin by saying that there is no rational reason why we should have hate crimes. Unfortunately, this world is a melting pot of all types of people. In the United States alone we have people believing that they are the superior race. For example look at the white supremacist groups and the skin heads. A change in the UCR mandated by the U.S. Congress for the collection of hate crimes statistics was a measuring tool for acquiring information on the different types of hate crimes that were committed in the United States. As a result of the initiation of the Hate Crime Statistics Act of 1990, the Federal Bureau of Investigation was required to start to collect the data on hate crimes. Hate crimes were broken down into categories, such as people with disabilities, people of a different race, religion, sexual and etc.

As mentioned above, the criminals that commit these crimes are individuals with a sense of superiority, religious fanatics, individuals against biracial relationships, and the KKK, etc. The victims of these crimes are usually African Americans, biracial families, homosexual individuals and the disabled. Let us keep in mind that these crimes are committed by cowards, individuals who are afraid or will not believe that all people are equal in the eyes of the law and humanity. These crimes are mostly committed at night or in the case of the KKK, in the south and at night. Also let us not forget how they keep their heads covered so that you can't identify them. In addition, we have the white supremacists that may not hide behind darkness, but they certainly hide behind the fact that they really feel a sense of insecurity.

According to research data, "the vast majorities of reported hate crimes are not committed by organized hate groups and their members, but by teenagers, primarily white males, acting alone or in a group". A child is not born with a hate gene. Hating is a learned behavior, it is something in which is learned from your immediate environment or from the friends you associate with during those informative years.

ANECDOTE

While working in Towson, Maryland I was introduced to racism from a very young bigot. One of my responsibilities was to relieve cashiers. After completing the task, it was time for me to take my lunch hour. I communicated this to the other cashiers. The next person in line at the register was a white female with her son. The little boy seemed to be about five years old. The child made a remark as I was leaving for lunch. "Go get the garbage truck". I was astonished by the remark. I couldn't believe that this remark was coming from a five year old child. It's been about forty-five years now since I experienced the incident. I remember saying to myself this is a learned behavior. The child's mother never said a word to her child about what he said. She just ignored the remark. I'm sharing this because that five year old may have grown up to commit a hate crime. What our children learn can be learned from their home environments. Hate is a learned behavior. That child could be one of our senators. That child could also be in one of our prisons by now because he decided to commit a hideous hate crime. The remark that the child made was not a hate crime according to the laws of society, however it was a serious crime because the child not only insulted me but he also opened himself up to future crimes. The child's parent did not realize that she was also contributing to her son's bad manners. We should also realize the old saying spare the rod - spoil the child.

What can we do to combat the problem of hate crimes? We can start with the immediate environment. The home environment would be the first place to start. We can attempt to initiate programs within the school systems. We could attempt to influence what is presented in the different types of media. We could attempt to include more detailed questions, regarding hate crimes in our U.S. Census Bureau surveys. "Do we have Census bureau Surveys anymore?"

After the creation of the UCR by the Federal Bureau of Investigation (FBI) in the early 1930's an effort was made to accurately define and keep track of statistics relating to the reporting of crime in the United States.

_____

_____

_____

_____

_____

_____

_____

_____

_____

CHAPTER TWO

CRIMINAL HOMICIDE

Criminal Homicide is defined as the willful killing of one human being by another, legal justification or excuse, according to UCR. UCR states, "The preferred term used by most law enforcement agencies is Criminal Homicide". Homicides are broken down into various categories, (1) first degree murder, which is usually premeditated and allegedly committed mostly by African American males; (2) second degree murder is defined as a homicide which is unplanned, an unlawful killing in which the intent to kill and the killing itself arise almost simultaneously, in the heat of passion." For instance, "a person who kills in a fit of anger is likely to be charged with second-degree murder. Usually a crime of passion is committed by a physically abused individual or out of an argument". Finally, third degree murder or negligent homicide is defined as a result of some other action, committed by a drunk driver, for instance. Another example of third degree murder could be called by an offender who attempts to rob a bank and as a result a customer of the bank gets killed in the process of the bank robbery. The UCR only measures the number of homicides committed. The victims of murders were suggested to be mostly young African American males and 92% of African American males were victims measured by the UCR. We can assume now that those statistics have changed due to the many violent crimes that are taking place in our schools and other places.

ANECDOTE

Keep in mind, that our prisons do have individuals who have been accused of crimes but never committed the crime and many years later was released because it was finally proven that the said individual was innocent after all. I personally am familiar with one individual associated with this stigma. After many years he has been found to be innocent and was released last year.

_____

_____

_____

_____

_____

_____

CHAPTER THREE

FORCIBLE RAPE

The crime of forcible rape is regarded as a personal crime because it is done in the present of the victim. It is all regarded as a violent crime because in some jurisdictions it is done with a weapon. The victims usually are females and at times males. A forcible rape does not include statutory rape. Statutory rape is the result of two consenting individuals but one being underage according to certain jurisdictions. There are several types of rapes, such as spousal rape, which are not always reported to the police. There is also date rape. This usually occurs on a date. Date Rape is defined as unlawful sexual intercourse. Powerless individuals who rape are seeking power. They usually prey on the weak individuals, those individuals with low self-esteem or those individuals who seem most vulnerable. Young girls are the most vulnerable according to the statistics by UCR.

CHAPTER FOUR

ROBBERY

The crime of robbery is regarded as a personal crime because it is done in the present of the victim. It is defined by the UCR Program as "the unlawful taking or attempted taking of property that is in the immediate possession of another by force or threat of force or violence and/or by putting the victim in fear." "Robberies generally occur most frequently in December. It is probably a reflection of an increased need for money and other goods around the holiday season". "The impact of this violent crime on its victims, according to UCR cannot be measured in terms of monetary loss alone"

The UCR further states, "Youths under the age of 18 accounted for offenders arrested in 28% of all robberies counted as cleared, and nearly two-thirds of all people apprehended for robbery were under 25 years of age." In addition, robberies indicate that a weapon is more likely used.

_____

_____

_____

_____

_____

_____

_____

_____

_____

_____

CHAPTER FIVE

AGGRAVATED ASSAULT

Aggravated Assault is regarded as a personal crime because it involves a personal insult on a victim intentionally, resulting in the victim obtaining bodily harm and possibly spending at least two days in the hospital. Usually, during the crime of aggravated assault weapons are used. "Under all programs assaults that cause serious bodily injury are scored as aggravated assaults." Statistics indicate that the highest number of aggravated assaults occur in the metropolitan areas and during the hot summer months, specifically July.

_____

_____

_____

_____

_____

_____

_____

CHAPTER SIX

BURGLARY

The crime of burglary is defined as the unlawful entry of a structure to commit a felony or a theft." "Burglary, according to UCR/NIBRS and NCVS is scored in three different categories. (1) Forcible entry, (2) attempted forcible entry and (3) unlawful entry where no force is used." Most burglaries were committed by men and were under the age of eighteen and were white. Reports indicate that most burglaries are higher among African American households. The report also indicates that African American families living in the city are more likely to have their homes burglarized. The reports also indicate that African American individuals living in rural areas are also more likely to have their homes burglarized than whites. Finally, burglaries according to reports have shown a decrease.

CHAPTER SEVEN

LARCENY/THEFT

The crime of larceny/theft is defined as the unlawful taking and attempting to carry, lead, or riding away of property from the possession or constructive possession of another. The larceny rate has increased somewhat in previous years. I suppose most victims of larceny/theft would be senior citizens, youths, vulnerable individuals and retail establishments. I would think that the larceny/theft is an all year crime, however mostly committed around the holidays and therefore would be on the rise.

CHAPTER EIGHT

MOTOR VEHICLE THEFT

A motor vehicle crime is defined as "the theft or attempted theft of a motor vehicle." According to the FBI, this offense category includes the stealing of automobiles, trucks, buses, motorcycles, motor scooters and snowmobiles." The taking of an automobile unlawfully is not always a crime, per se. For instance a spouse taking a car without the consent of his or her spouse is not a crime which is reported to the FBI by the police. The reason being is because in most jurisdictions, most married couples own property together. Then, however, you have carjacking, which is defined as a much more serious crime because it is usually committed with a victim in the car or is threatened with a weapon. "Carjacking increased rapidly in the early 1990s, when thieves targeted vehicles that could be sold easily for valuable parts", according to FBI statistics. FBI states, that August is the prime month for car theft and occur in cities.

CHAPTER NINE

ARSON

Arson is defined as "the willful or malicious burning or attempt to burn, with or without intent to defraud, of a dwelling house, public building, motor vehicle or aircraft, personal property of another, etc." The offenders in the case of arson could be an individual who is in financial need, a person who just merely likes to start fires and possibly vandals, etc. The FBI states that in 2006, arson arrest involved juveniles. "Seventy-six (76%) percent of arson arrestees were white and eighty-three (83%) percent were men.

At this point I don't know if I can elaborate on what I would do to improve the reporting of crime. It seems that the FBI and other reporting agencies are doing the best they can under the circumstances. It appears that the crime rate in all eight crimes on the UCR list has increased over the last couple of years. I would attempt to decrease those numbers. I would also attempt to fine tune the data gathering for the reports. I would monitor the police more effectively to make sure that all crimes are being reported. I would also incorporate into insurance applications surveys to identify at risks persons who may be inclined to commit arson for the insurance money.

CHAPTER TEN

CRIMES AGAINST PERSONS

O n a personal note, I am familiar with bullying. Bullying happens to those individuals that others believe are quiet and who are not capable of defending themselves. As a teenager I was quiet. As a result I got harassed. I always found myself defending myself because I was quiet. Today, society considers this type of harassment as bullying. Fortunately, these so called bullies discovered that just because I was quiet it did not mean that I would tolerate their bullying. As a result I found myself in fights after school. It was not until I got suspended from school and had to face the raft of my mother that I learned that defending myself with my fists was not the answer. From that day forward I began to utilize my intellect to defend myself. I thought that sharing this with my readers that it could help anyone who has a bullying problem. We find bullies in all walks of life. So, it is a crime at any age, but unfortunately it seems that nothing is legally done until bullying gets out of hand. Bullying is considered a "crime against another individual." Stay tuned for the more sophisticated crimes.

ANECDOTE

On another personal note, my family lived on a fairly quiet street in North Philadelphia. My family was not rich nor poor, perhaps you can say that we had a comfortable life. We did not go without meals and always had clean clothing. We had what we called our Sunday go to meeting clothing, Easter we got new outfits. Well, this one Sunday, my older brother did not change out of his Sunday clothing and he asked if he could go to the corner store. He was granted permission, but he did not know what awaited him that day. Unfortunately, when he came out of the store some bullies were waiting for him. They made my brother strip out of his new clothes and my brother had to come home without his clothing. This was a turning point in my brother's life. He swore that day that no one would ever bully him again. Soon, thereafter my brother would never back down from a confrontation. He was never to be bullied again. I share these truths with you in this book because I want you to have some understanding of how our youths take the difficult road and end up in trouble. My brother was ultimately shamed that day to his soul. I suppose that my parents could have attempted to guide him in a different direction – I just don't know. I suppose that we all may have been bullied at some point in life – but who is to know. And, how was the situation handled?

CHAPTER ELEVEN

INSTITUTIONAL CRIME

ANECDOTE

On Thursday, February 18, 2010 a disenchanted an angry, AJS, 3rd of Austin, Texas, before leaving his home set his house on fire, drove his car to the Georgetown Municipal Airport where he kept a small plane, flew it into a building killing himself and one other person, who worked in the building.

The crime data suggests that this is a crime in which we can refer to as an "Institutional Crime". The textbook defines an "Institutional Crime" as "a goal-directed offense that involves some degree of planning by the defender."

Referencing the article published by the msnbc.com staff and news service reports, AJS was upset with the Service. It would seem that anger would be a strong motive behind this crime. AJS expressed his feelings of discontent on his company website the day of the crime. Following is an excerpt from the message posted on the company website. "If you're reading this, you're no doubt asking yourself, 'Why did this have to happen?' The simple truth is that it is complicated and has been coming for a long time." (www.msn.com/id/35460268/ns/us_news-life)

It is obvious that AJS had been planning this crime for some time now. AJS was so overwhelmed with anger over losing a great deal of his money, which he felt was the fault of the Company. Not only does this crime indicate planning, which makes it an "Institutional Crime"; it also has signs of a person making terrorist threats directed toward employees. Note, he did not single one particular individual or individuals, but the threat was made toward the company. One can infer that "Domestic Terrorism" was indicative of his actions. Domestic Terrorism is defined as, "The unlawful use of force or violence by a group or an individual who is based and operates entirely within the United States and its territories without foreign direction and whose acts are directed at elements of the U.S. Government or population."

There was definitely a connection between the type of crime and the location of the crime. In AJS's mind, he blamed the Company for his financial problems. According to the article he lost quite a bit of money. AJS felt the only way to let the Company feel his anger and show the Company how serious he was AJS wanted to destroy the very source of his anger – which was the Company. This was definitely an act of terrorism - which is a crime. The crime was premeditated violence and politically motivated. Moreover, it was intended to influence others. "Violence is the only answer," was the message communicated on AJS's website.

What prevention strategies could have been employed to reduce this type of crime? Good question! I am not sure whether this could have been prevented or not. We will never know fully what really happened between the Company and AJS. AJS is no longer here to defend his position. Who would have known that AJS was planning such a crime? Perhaps the Company might consider reevaluating their procedures on how they might deal with angry and disenchanted citizens. Or, could the Company be considered a bully?

_____

_____

_____

_____

_____

_____

_____

CHAPTER TWELVE

TRUE STORY

ANECDOTE

We never stop to realize how our work environment affects our lives. Working in the midst of discrimination and racism is a nightmare. High school was the last time I experienced discrimination and racism. There were fights in the streets, name calling, students being suspended and going to jail. Not only did I learn about this in high school but I lived through it in my neighborhood of West Oak Lane. We were the only black family on our block in West Oak Lane. The neighbors did not want to live next to us. I witnessed families moving out one by one until it was just the neighbors on either side of our home - two Jewish families. My family survived through the prejudice, but the damage was embedded in myself and my siblings. It is important to note that I was about fourteen at the time.

Those years were very impressionable for me and my siblings. Time was spent worrying about being safe. I felt that my education and guidance was extremely hindered as a result of the hatred. I once had a counselor who convinced me that I was not college material. This stayed with me throughout adulthood. I was a shy teenager who had the responsibility of watching over my younger siblings. In addition, I had the responsibility of cleaning and cooking for the family. I had little time for study. Nevertheless, I made it through high school with little studying. I was an average student, but I knew I could do better, if given the opportunity. As a result of my low self-esteem during those impressionable years - I didn't pursue college. I graduated high school and entered the workforce. I have been working ever since.

In 1994 I stopped working for other businesses and started my own business. I incorporated all that I had learned throughout the years from working for others under my own business umbrella. I don't want to get that far ahead of myself. However, in 1980 I entered Community College of Philadelphia and achieved a degree in Journalism. Community College of Philadelphia helped me to achieve the confidence I so desperately needed. My confidence began to grow stronger. I left that low self-esteem behind. I finally became an "A" student at CCP. I noticed that as long as I had other responsibilities my grades would decline. When I made school my priority I received good grades. That stigma of not being college material was beginning to fade away. Getting back to the years of managing my own business, business was great up until the economy started to shift. I found myself looking for temporary work to make ends meet.

It was during this time that God directed my steps to a law firm in Delaware County. It was here that I, once again, started to experience racism and bigotry. I have been at this firm for eleven years and it seems as though I am back in the 60's. I allowed myself to get comfortable in the job. I began to get bored with what I was doing. There is no opportunity for advancement. If I showed any type of initiative it was not good. All the supervisors I had previously spoke very highly of me. They liked the idea that I showed initiative when it came to my duties. I also had the opportunity to utilize my writing skills in other positions. Once I started getting bored I enrolled in the University to obtain a degree in criminal justice. The reason for this decision, I felt it was time to give back to the community. I would see more and more of a revolving door of our youths – where prison played a substantial part in their upbringing. I wanted to do something worthwhile. I graduated from the University with honors. The firm never even acknowledged this accomplishment.

It was around 9:45 a.m., feeling dizzy, I cautiously walked to my car. I had no clue, "What is happening to me", I mumbled. I was wobbly, but I reached my car hoping to steady myself. "Sitting here in my car, I cautiously drove home. By the time I reached home I was feeling much better. This was not the first time I had this scare. Once, in the supermarket and once before at the firm. I knew what it was – it was stress. Now, it is time to share with you what led up to this particular incident.

Approximately, about a month ago I needed to obtain some additional file cabinets for my office. It was revealed to me by another secretary that there were some extra file cabinets in her area and that she would ask her boss if I can have them. She informed me that her boss was out of the office that particular day and would return to the office the next day and she would ask him then. I normally get in early around 8:30 a.m., she also arrived early, usually before me. Additionally, her boss arrives early as well. I noticed that the attorney was in the office early that morning so I took the opportunity to approach him in regards to obtaining the file cabinets. The attorney said that I could get the file cabinets because there were also two more that were not being utilized. I called the individual whom we contracted to do odd jobs around the office and he came and moved the files to my area. During the movement of the files the secretary noticed that it was being taken care of and she thanked me sarcastically. I told her she was welcomed. From that day forward she did not speak to me because she felt that I did not wait for her to get permission from her boss. The truth of the matter was that I saw an opportunity to get the job done. There was not any reason that I could see why she did not ask him when he arrived in that morning.

Furthermore, my files were so tight that each time I attempted to put away files I would get paper cuts on my hands. I needed to get filing done and she procrastinated. I believe that this was done deliberately. I am not a favorite person in the eyes of others at the firm. So, given the opportunity, my efforts to solve a problem would be sabotaged.

Going forward, I noticed that one of the attorney's began to treat me differently. I was having a problem with seeing the wording on the computer when I was working on the computer. I attempted to try to make the font larger but could not accomplish the task. I approached the bookkeeper about the matter and she could not handle the matter appropriately. She directed me to her supervisor. He attempted to help but to no avail.

When he was leaving I asked what he was going to do about the problem. He informed me that he asked the bookkeeper to contact the Company. I later asked if she had done so and she informed me that she did but later recanted and said that her supervisor did not say to call. In the meantime I was concerned about the procrastination because my eyes were in jeopardy. I began to research the matter and came across an email address for the helpline for the Company. I informed the bookkeeper telling her that I would send an email. She said okay. When I got a response I informed the bookkeeper of the response and I told her that I would send her a copy of the email and she informed me to send one to her supervisor. I did, not knowing that I was being setup. The supervisor was furious. He gave me a tongue lashing as though I was a child. He did not allow me to say anything – he cut me off by saying, "It is the end of the conversation." The above is just a small part of how I was treated. Again, on previous positions elsewhere, my supervisors had no problem with me showing initiative. I felt and still feel this firm is antiquated in how they function. It is like living in the "60s" once again. They wish that I, according to them, to stay in my place "below them". This will never happen. I perceive the above examples of how an employee is mistreated as a result of one's color. How did the incidents make me feel? Whatever I would do or say it did not matter and that it was not worth the effort. It made me feel that I was not part of the team. In order for a team to work properly all team players should be involved working for the success of the team. I am made to feel alienated. That is not a good way to feel. Finally, I wanted to give up trying to be part of the team.

CHAPTER THIRTEEN

CYBER BULLYING

Cyber Bullying is somewhat of a new type of crime. Cyber bullying happens a lot among youths today. If a youth do not fit into a certain type of group he or she may find themselves being bullied by the so called popular teens. If the said youth is shy and withdrawn he or she may not be able to withstand the harassment he or she is subjected to. In some cases these youths are drawn to committing murder. A good example of the retaliation is the shootings on various campuses as well as high schools. We need to take the time to listen to our youths, especially if we know that our youths are somewhat quiet and withdrawn. We should not be so busy working at our jobs and businesses that we allow our children to attempt to solve his or her problems alone. As we can see the result may be murder or the taking of his or her own life. What do we have then to live with – the loss of a child?

Cyber bullying is not the only means of bullying. Our children have access to social media, television and other means of bullying. Cyber bullying opened the door to the negative communication. It creates an atmosphere for negative communication and its not only up to the parents to attempt to put a stop to it all but the public as well. We have control of how we allow our children to utilize computers, what they watch on television, what movies that they go to and who they socialize with at times.

CHAPTER FOURTEEN

GRIMES AGAINST PROPERTY

On February 22, 2010 AF, 43, of Glen Mills, Pennsylvania and his brother DF were sentenced to twenty-eight (28) months in prison for a kickback scheme which involved the Credit Union located in Pennsylvania; where AF was employed as Vice President and Marketing Director. AF implemented a scheme to provide and approve loans for unqualified applicants, according to the U.S. Attorney. November 2009, AF pleaded guilty to the scheme in which he and his brother DF netted about $100,000 in kickbacks from more than $2.2 million in fraudulent loans, reported by the Philadelphia Inquirer. (Issue: Feb. 22, 2010, the Philadelphia Inquirer).

The difficulty in proving the crime was because AF did such a good job in concealing his criminal actions. Evidently he must have some knowledge of accounting. The problem is that white-collar criminals are usually very intelligent and can manipulate records and conceal the crime unless they are frequently audited. With this type of crime AF would have to be investigated over a period of time.

In addition, these types of criminals can hire the best defense attorneys and sometimes just get away with a slap on the risk and a fine, depending upon how serious the crime is. U.S. District Court Judge took into account at sentencing, the fact that the younger brother, DF has been diagnosed with a malignant brain tumor, as stated by the U.S. Attorney's office. (Issue: Feb. 22, 2010, Delaware County Daily Times). The Sarbanes-Oxley Act in 2002 (a.k.a., the Public Company Accounting Reform and Investor Protection Act) was passed with "the goal of making it easier for investigators and prosecutors to navigate the murky waters of corporate crime. The Sarbanes-Oxley Act states that stiff penalties are set for CEO's and CFO's and required them to vouch for the truth of their companies' financial disclosures."

AF is not a CEO or CFO; however his supervisors are still responsible for his actions. On the other hand, AF was definitely motivated by old fashion greed. AF used his position as an executive vice president and marketing director at the Credit Union to facilitate the issuance of the loans to unqualified applicants in exchange for the kickbacks. He then recruited his brother, DF who worked as a maintenance worker for the credit union to find applicants for his scheme.

There is definitely a connection between the type of crime and the location of the crime. We can surmise that it could be characterized as a white-collar crime because of the location and the position of the individual. The nature of the crime suggests crime against property and we can reference it as an "Occupational Crime". "Any act punishable by law that is committed through opportunity created in the course of an occupation that is illegal." (Criminology Today, Page 494). AF benefited personally in the crime. The crime was committed at AF's place of employment with him using his office as a means to a fortune. And being that AF was a vice president and marketing director he was in a prime position to commit such a crime. How AF's actions went undetected for so long is a mystery. Most financial institutions adhere to financial audits periodically to combat this type of crime.

In retrospect, it is important to implement strategies in order to combat problems of fraud in most financial institutions. There should always be checks and balances. An audit once a year to examine the financial records of the institution would have been sufficient. In an Article written by B.R. Farrell, 1999 stated that the following information should be the responsibility of an auditor. "The auditor has a responsibility to plan and perform the audit to obtain reasonable assurance about whether the financial statements are free of material misstatement, whether caused by error or fraud."

_____

_____

_____

_____

SECTION TWO

THE NEGATIVE AND POSITIVE EFFECT OF ETHICS IN SOCIETY

CHAPTER FIFTEEN

ETHICS, LEADERSHIP AND CRIMINAL JUSTICE

Aristotle's Virtues

Courage: a police officer apprehending two armed suspects; **Temperance:** a police officer not being over-zealous while performing his duties; **Liberality:** a police officer being tolerant of other ethnic groups; **Magnificence:** a police officer donating time and money to a youth group; **Proper Pride:** CP who takes pride in performing his duties; **Gentleness:** a compassionate police officer who is caring and gentle when it comes to performing his duties; **Friendliness:** a police officer who patrols a community regularly and is courteous and friendly toward the people in the community; **Righteous Indignation:** a police officer observing another officer accepting a bribe; **Truthfulness:** a police officer who is above reproach; **Wittiness:** a police officer who is pleasant and amusing; **Modesty:** a police officer who sets a good example for the community.

What is the difference between ethics and morality? Ethics is dealing with principles we all live by in our professional lives – a moral code as such. For example, a doctor who has taken the "the Hippocratic Oath", which is an oath taken by doctors swearing to practice medicine ethically. The following is an excerpt from "The Oath of Hippocrates." "I will follow that system of regimen which, according to my ability and judgment, I consider for the benefit of my patients, and abstain from whatever is deleterious and mischievous. I will give no deadly medicine to any one if asked, nor suggest any such counsel; and in like manner I will not give to a woman a pessary to produce abortion." (http://www.doctorslounge.com/oath.htm).

A good example is Dr. Jack Kevorkian who helped terminally ill patients to die. He violated his Hippocratic Oath. Hence, it was ethically wrong.

ETHICAL DECISION MAKING

"You are a police officer patrolling a fairly remote area near the coast line during a fast approaching storm and tidal surge. You receive an urgent radio message that a woman and five small children are stranded on a beach near your patrol area. There is a 10 minute window to reach them before they face certain doom. The only way to get to them with the time available is with your car. However, the road narrows between two cliffs to the width of a single vehicle, and there is no way around. As you approach you notice a man with his leg stuck in a crack in the middle of the road between the cliffs. You determine you cannot help him as it will take the fire department and EMS to free him. What are you going to do?" (Singh, 2010).

ACTUAL TRUE STORY

Let us consider this scenario. You are a notary public working in a law firm practicing in Pennsylvania. Notaries are bound by laws set forth in the State of Pennsylvania. In the State of Pennsylvania a Notary is not allowed to notarize a document without the person he or she is performing the act is not present. In this scenario, the Notary is approached by an attorney to notarize and back date a document and the person is not there and he or she has never met the person. This is definitely against the laws of the State of Pennsylvania. And, in this case the firm in which he or she works can be fined by the State

30

of Pennsylvania. The attorney who requested that the Notary violate this law is in breach of his or her integrity as an attorney of the State of Pennsylvania. These papers in which I am sharing with you are met to reveal how in certain circumstances our youths can go astray. The act of the attorney and the notary in this instance will have a derogatory effect on everyone involved. First, there are two other notaries in this firm. One, of which works directly with the attorney in question. The attorney did not approach the notary that works with him because he knows that the notary would not agree to notarize the document because it would prove to be an illegal act. So, he went to the notary that he knew would not question his action because he knows she would accommodate him to stay in the good graces of the partners of the firm. As a result the notary who would not break the law would not be favored by the partners of the firm, resulting in passed over for increases in salary as well as anything else favorable. This scenario is just another example of what goes on in society and how it effects the lifestyle of others.

What is Ethical Decision-Making? "Ethical decision-making consists of two levels of moral reasoning, the intuitive level, which consists of personal feelings and the right and wrong of a situation. The second consists of the evaluative level. This involves judgment and evaluations of the situation. That being said consider the first abovementioned scenario. Is there truly an ethical issue with this situation? Yes! I, as an officer of the law have an ethical responsibility to do whatever it takes to save the mother and the five small children as well as the man stuck between the two cliffs. After obtaining all the facts I would determine that the best way in helping everyone involved would be to utilize the "Utilitarian Approach", which would result in the most good and the least harm to everyone concerned. (Williams & Arrigo, 2008).

I would call dispatch for assistance requesting the help of the fire department and EMS to rescue the man. I would also request assistance from the Coast Guard to rescue the mother and the five small children because it would be impossible for me to get to them in time. Accordingly, my decision as an officer of the law would demonstrate good decision making because I have managed both situations and respected their individual rights as citizens to be rescued, which would be a demonstration of the "Right Base Approach" as well as the "Fairness Approach". What the Right Base Approach means in this situation is that I would have respected everyone involved in the situation. As citizens within my jurisdiction, they were in a vulnerable situation which demanded immediate assistance.

The "Fairness Approach", which means that everyone concerned was treated fairly in the situation.

(Swinton). I am concerned about every person's dilemma and would proceed to get help for all involved. Above all as an officer of the law I demonstrated quick thinking of the situation and this indicates what kind of values I have as well as my character, strengths and courage to make the right ethical decision. This speaks to the "Virtue Approach". According to Swinton, "our ethical actions should be consistent with certain ideal virtues that help to develop each individual's full development where humanity is concerned." (Swinton).

Moreover, in calling for additional rescue for both the man and the family it indicated good judgment and a high degree of morality. I was not thinking of myself at the time, just the individuals in question, no self-interest, therefore I acted with little egoism by putting the needs of the man as well as the family first in solving the problem at hand. There were no immediate rewards for me except for knowing that the emergency situation was handled ethically and morally. All in a day's work!

In retrospect, I would have definitely put myself and the others in harm's way if I had not made the call and attempted to reach the family by foot, which would have possibly resulted in negative consequences for everyone. In addition, the decision to make the calls to the police dispatch center for assistance was an excellent example of "Ethical Decision-Making". I had to think quickly. I was given the facts. I made the best decision under the circumstances.

In summarizing, making good ethical decisions requires a trained sensitivity to ethical issues. Police officers are trained for situations such as the scenario mentioned above. In addition, "The Common Good Approach" exemplifies good ethical reasoning in law enforcement by the simple fact that the "interlocking relationships of society are the basis of ethical reasoning and that respect and compassion for all others-especially the vulnerable-are requirements of law enforcement". (Swinton).

ETHICS AND LEADERSHIP

This paper will discuss meta-ethics, normative ethics and applied ethics. But before discussing meta-ethics, normative ethics we need to understand the meaning of ethics and understand that meta-ethics, normative ethics and applied ethics are an extension of ethics. "Ethics is two things. First, ethics refers to well-founded standards of right and wrong that prescribe what humans ought to do, usually in terms of rights, obligations, benefits to society, fairness, or specific virtues. Secondly, ethics refers to the study and development of one's ethical standards." (Velasquez, Andre, Shanks, S.J., and Meyer, 2010).

Let us begin with meta-ethics, which "talks about the nature of ethics and moral reasoning. Metaethics are discussions about whether ethics is relative and whether we always act from self-interest, these are examples of meta-ethical discussions." (New World Encyclopedia). Consider this scenario. Two people are in a discussion about right or wrong, both attempting to prove a point, the discussion gets pretty heated and they don't make any progress on the issue being debated. Basically they are both saying the same thing but utilizing different words. Consider this scenario, meta-ethics is not interested in who is right or wrong. Metaethics is only concerned with the analysis of the terms right or wrong. Let us consider another scenario. Two brothers have a sister who is terminally ill. The discussion is on euthanasia. One brother believes it is wrong to take the sister's life. The other feels that it is humane to end her life. They get nowhere in their discussion. Metaethics studies the nature of ethics, not who was right or wrong. (New World Encyclopedia).

Moreover, normative ethics "is interested in determining the content of our moral behavior. Normative ethical theories seek to provide action-guides; procedures for answering the practical question ("What ought I to do")." Let us consider the issue of euthanasia once again. "Normative ethics, also known as normative theory is concerned with which actions are right or wrong. Hence, is it right or wrong to end a terminally ill person's life? In addition, "It intends to find out which character traits are good and bad." (New World Encyclopedia). Normative ethics are also concerned with the moral issue of normative ethics. Consider the work of Jeremy Bentham, an English philosopher and political radical. Bentham was known for his moral philosophy, "especially his principle of utilitarianism, which evaluates actions based upon their consequences". (Sweet, 2008). In other words, how do the consequences of the action affect the happiness of all individuals affected by the action?

Yet, applied ethics "attempts to deal with specific realms of human action and to craft criteria for discussing issues that might arise within those realms." (Joseph, 2000). In addition, dealing with such topics as business ethics, medical ethics, computer ethics, just to name a few. "There are generally two approaches taken in applied ethics. The first is to apply ethical principles such as utilitarianism and deontological ethics to each issue or question; the second is to generate a situation-based discourse that uses multiple ethical theories". In addition, the result of a recent national study provide solid data that leaders who want to establish a practice of positive workplace ethics standards, provide ethics training, and ensure resources are available for employees in need of ethics advice." (Joseph, 2000). Consider this scenario, discrimination in a law firm. We know that discrimination of any kind is illegal in the workplace, let alone a law firm. Of all work environments, applied ethics should be actively pursued. For a law firm to be practicing discrimination is not only illegal, but unethical.

In summarizing this paper, let us look at ethics as being the nucleus for meta-ethics, which discusses the nature of ethics. On the other hand, normative ethics determines the content of moral behavior within the realm of normative ethics. Finally, applied ethics deals with the action of humans regarding particular issues and discussing those issues. Meta-ethics, normative ethics and applied ethics all are an extension of ethics.

CHAPTER SIXTEEN

LEADERSHIP SKILLS FOR THE CRIMINAL JUSTICE PROFESSION

Ethics and virtues are components of leadership skills in any profession which should be practiced, maintained and developed in our professional and personal lives. For criminal justice professionals ethics and virtues are vital in the development and maintenance of good leadership skills, as well as being able to adapt to change. According to Seymour (1998), "if there is one thing leaders can count on facing, it is change."

This country is constantly changing and our leaders in all criminal justice professions and other professions should be able to change along with society in an effort to improve on its professions. Moreover, every profession should have a sense of professionalism when performing the duties of the profession. In order for criminal justice professionals to maintain professionalism in carrying out the functions of his or her duties they must have knowledge of the job and good communications skills, as well. As a result of job knowledge, comes confidence in carrying out those duties, resulting in good ethical decision making, patience and tolerance for the individuals he or she comes in contact with on a daily basis, especially offenders of the law.

Most importantly, the criminal justice professional should have good organizational skills, "knowing how to set priorities", "good team building skills" and above all, a high degree of integrity, which includes "good principles, accountability, avoiding cover-ups", i.e., the taking of bribes – having the courage to speak up against misconduct and cover-ups. (Dodson, n.d.) This behavior should not only be included in a criminal justice professional's life but in his or her personal life as well.

ETHICS AND VIRTUE

Let us examine the importance of ethics and virtue in criminal justice leadership. A criminal justice professional should at all times respect the code of conduct. In the criminal justice professional field, (i.e.), police, lawyers, parole officer and judges, etc., each area has its own expertise, thereby having its own "code of ethics unique to that particular area. All codes of conduct, however, demand high ethical standards," states Al Vick, eHow Contributor. (Vick 2010).

According to Williams and Arrigo (2008), "virtue ethics emphasizes moral character, the embodiment of virtue in one's decisions and actions, and the avoidance of vice." Consider this example. An attorney asks a notary public to notarize documents that are already signed and dated by his client. This is illegal and unethical on the part of the attorney, according to Act 152 of the Notary Law. (2002). By asking the notary to notarize the document the attorney is asking him or her to break the law. At this point the moral and ethical character of the attorney is revealed by the decision he has made and resulting in an unlawful action on the part of the attorney.

To summarize, the above scenario is just one example of when ethics and virtue may come into play in any given field of criminal justice professionals. Criminal justice professionals must maintain and develop a high standard of professional conduct at all times no matter what the circumstances. Having good leadership skills includes demonstrating good ethics, virtues and moral behavior resulting in good characteristics in criminal justice professionals, resulting in a profession that people can respect and count on to protect and serve the public.

CHAPTER SEVENTEEN

MORAL DEVELOPMENT THEORY

ETHICS, CRIME AND CRIMINAL JUSTICE

On May 13, 1985 the Philadelphia police engaged in an unnecessary gun battle to serve warrants on four members of the "Move" organization at their communal residence located at 6221 Osage Avenue in the Powelton Village section of Philadelphia. The failed gun battle resulted in the police dropping a bomb on the residence, which ultimately destroyed 61 homes and also resulted in the death of six adults and five children. The entire incident was a horrendous lapse of ethical judgment by management of the Philadelphia Police Department and the Mayor of Philadelphia.

In an effort to understand what led up to this event it will be necessary to give a brief history of the MOVE organization, which was formed in Philadelphia, Pennsylvania in 1972 by Vincent Leaphart (a.k.a. John Africa) and Donald Glassey. It was then called the "American Christian Movement". Soon thereafter the group adopted a "back-to-nature lifestyle." The group preached living on the land and preached against the utilization of technology. As a result of the groups lifestyle they began to be scrutinized by members of the Philadelphia Police Department and resented by their neighbors.

"For a short period after moving into the Powelton village house, things were relatively quiet as MOVE kept to themselves" as stated in an article on libcom.org Internet Services. To the contrary, complaints from the neighbors indicated that MOVE was a "radical cult-like group that preached revolution, advocating a return to nature and a society without government, police or technology." (Sullivan 2005). Without going into further detail, why was there a lapse of ethical judgment on the part of the Philadelphia Police Department? What would Lawrence Kohlberg think of this situation? The primary participant in this tragic incident was John Africa and his followers and the Philadelphia Police Department officers (rogue police offers).

PRECONVENTIONAL MORALITY THEORY

Stage 1 - Obedience and Punishment Orientation

According to Kolberg, at this stage some might believe that the police should not have dropped a bomb on the MOVE communal. It was neither the ethical or moral thing to do. The police was not thinking about what would be best for the people within the communal, as well as the surrounding homes. John Africa and his followers had little respect for the law so they did not surrender to the police when asked to come out of the communal. This demonstrated a lack of the cognitive thought process. They did not think about the outcome of the situation.

Stage 2 – Individualism and Exchange

At this stage Kolhberg states, "Each person is free to pursue his or her individual interests". (Crain 1985). This was not acceptable for the neighbors of Osage Avenue. The MOVE individuals felt that it was their right to live the lifestyle that they chose. The police did not want to recognize this as their right, nor did they want to respect the right of the MOVE people to live their lives as individuals because it was different from theirs. Because of the fact that they perceived life to be much simpler - living naturally without technology it made them outcasts.

CONVENTIONAL MORALITY

Stage 3 - Good Interpersonal Relationship

The MOVE people were not conforming to the lifestyle in which the people of Powelton village believed that they should be living. As a result there were no good interpersonal relationships with the MOVE people, the police or the neighbors. The police were inundated with complaints from the citizens of Powelton village to the point where they just wanted to put an end to what they saw was a hostile situation. The MOVE people unsuccessfully tried to communicate their beliefs through various media but it fell on death ears. The people of Powelton village believed that the MOVE people did not have any respect for the community, no empathy and no concern for others.

Stage 4 – Maintaining the Social Order

At Stage 4, Kolhberg suggests that "the respondent becomes more broadly concerned with society as a whole." (Crain 1985). The respondent in this case would be MOVE - did they break any laws? In the beginning there were no laws broken. As time progressed and the MOVE agenda began to progress they would be cited for disturbing the peace. However, according to media the police began to arrest members of MOVE for no apparent reason. Soon thereafter MOVE demanded the release of their members. The situation changed from a non-violent movement to a violent movement.

POSTCONVENTIONAL MORALITY

Stage 5 – Social Contract and Individual Rights

According to Kohlberg, people are supposed to "recognize that different social groups within a society will have different values," but this was not the case in Powelton village in 1985. The Philadelphia Police Department and Powelton village neighbors of the MOVE communal believed that MOVE did not have the right to the lifestyle that they chose to live. MOVE did not have basic rights – their rights were not protected by the Police. The MOVE people who lost their lives in the bombing - were their rights protected under the same laws as the neighbors? Kohlberg mentions that under stage 4 "subjects frequently talk about the "right to life……." (Crain 1985).

Stage 6 – Universal Principles

Kolhberg insists that our principles should be universal. Kohlberg also suggests that "we can reach just decisions by looking at a situation through one another's eyes." Did the Philadelphia Police Department, the Mayor and Powelton village neighbors try to look at the MOVE situation through their eyes? The decision to drop the bomb at 6221 Osage Avenue on May 13, 1985 was definitely a lapse in ethical and moral judgment. In trying to defuse a situation it resulted in one of the worse decisions in the history of the Philadelphia Police Department. It just made a bad situation worse. There was little forethought and very little managing of the situation. Lives and homes were lost in the process and it cost the city more to rebuild the neighborhood. And that day in May will forever be in the memories of the citizens of Philadelphia, Pennsylvania and surrounding areas.

In summarizing, Kolhberg's theory on the stages of moral development is more apparent in the development of children, however when you are applying it to a situation such as the MOVE situation we need to rethink the theory - do we all evolve and develop morally as we should? As we develop through the stages our behavior and cognitive thought process should also develop as well, resulting in better ethical and moral decision making. As far as the various stages of individuals, John Africa seemed to be in stage 5, reason being because he was fighting for the individual rights of his fellow MOVE members. Just to live in peace. As for the police they seem to be at stage 4 trying to maintain the social order of the community. As for the people of Powelton village they were at stage 4 - their concern was with society as a whole, particularly, their neighborhood. They were concerned with MOVE destroying the neighborhood as a result of MOVE's lifestyle. Ultimately, all participants destroyed the neighborhood.

PHILOSOPHICAL APPROACHES

This paper will discuss and define two philosophical approaches, one of which is Legal Moralism and the other, Legal Paternalism. It will give explanations of each approach as it relates to the criminal justice professional. The paper will show how both approaches are similar, yet in how both approaches vary in differences. In the discussion scenarios will be presented to further demonstrate the philosophical approaches. Upon completion of the discussion, it will be noted which approach is preferable to me and why.

Legal Moralism as it is defined by the Internet Encyclopedia of Philosophy (IEP) states that, "Legal Moralism is the view that the law can legitimately use to prohibit behaviors that conflict with society's collective moral judgments" (Hart 1963). Consider this scenario. You have a twenty-one year old man and a fifteen year old girl who are in love. They want to consummate their love by sex, yet the laws in the United States prevent them from doing so because the young man is of age and the girl is not. However, the two engage in love making to consummate their love for each other but the family discovers what they have done. The family reports the young man to the authority and he is quickly charged with statutory rape. "In accordance with the FBI definition, statutory rape is characterized as non-forcible sexual intercourse with a person who is younger than the statutory age of consent." (sexlaw.org). In some countries, such as South Africa the legal age is sixteen for sexual activity. In the US it goes against the normality of our society's laws. H.L.A. Hart (1963) said, "A society can survive a diversity of behavior in many other areas of moral concern-as is evidenced by the controversies in the U.S. surrounding abortion and homosexuality."

Secondly, according to IEP, Legal Paternalism is defined as "Is the view that it is permissible for the state to legislate against individuals who they think are conflicting harm or danger to themselves or others." Consider this scenario. A rich senior citizens travels to an economically deprived section of the city he begins distributing cash to the poor. His actions are discovered by his family, they believe that he has become incompetent. As a result, they attempt to have him committed. The senior wanted to give back to the community in which helped him to acquire his wealth. In giving away his money in this manner caused him to put himself and others in harms' way, even though his intentions were good. Yet, it is his right to do what he wanted with his money. Karl Rabeder, millionaire gave away money because it made him miserable. (Jones 2010). Someone without money would not say this. Is Rabeder incompetent?

Both these approaches impact criminal justice professionals by the mere fact that the criminal justice professional, i.e. police officers and judges must enter the picture by taking the young man in the first scenario in custody and in the second scenario, the senior will be taken into custody to determine by the courts that he is competent. In cases such as the above scenarios, criminal justice professionals are involved in a courtroom environment.

The approaches are similar because in both scenarios the individual right to freely live according to their own beliefs are violated, but not according to society's laws. Which approach is better? I will go with the Legal Paternalism Approach. In today's society, one cannot be too careful. The Legal Paternalism Approach is good because it protects some of the good hearted people in these United States, whereas the Legal Moralism Approach hinders freedom of expression.

In summary, the criminal justice professionals can give guidance and counseling in this area as to what families can do to prevent these types of situations. Committing individuals to hospitals and incarceration of individuals is not always the correct alternative. Both philosophical approaches should be analyzed to work more efficiently to better serve the public.

_____

_____

_____

_____

_____

_____

_____

_____

_____

_____

CHAPTER EIGHTEEN

THE ROLE OF INTEGRITY IN CRIMINAL JUSTICE WORK

What is the relevancy of integrity in the position of a judge in the criminal justice system? What role does integrity play in the work of a criminal justice judge? We must understand the true meaning of the word integrity. The Oxford American Dictionary defines integrity as being "honest, incorruptible, wholeness, entirety and soundness. Exactly what does this mean to a criminal judge? (Ehrlich, E., Flexner S.B., Carruth, G., Hawkins, J.M. 1980).

The Code of Judicial Conduct states that a judge "shall personally observe high standards of conduct so that the integrity and independence of the judiciary may be preserved". (Code of Judicial Conduct 2005).

Just consider the power that a judge has in his profession. He holds a criminal's fate in his hands and he is also in the position to help to rehabilitate criminals, give reduced sentences to criminals, probation, or the death penalty. In the lives of criminal offenders who have been found guilty and is waiting to hear their sentence this means the difference between life and death, depending on the crime.

A judge's position is a position that should be incorruptible. In order for this to be a reality in the life of a judge he should first be honest with himself and confident that he will make the right ethical decision always. Judges are no different than the layman. Judges have weaknesses as any other person, thereby capable of breaking the law.

Additionally, in an effort to avoid corruption a judge's personal life should be squeaky clean. There should not be any skeletons in the closet in which corrupt individuals can uncover to blackmail a judge to influence his decision on sentencing or his actions during a trial. A judge's life should be open to complete scrutiny - wholeness as such. (Ehrlich, E., Flexner S.B., Carruth, G., Hawkins, J.M. 1980).

Finally, according to the Code of Judicial Conduct (CJC) a judge should always "avoid impropriety and the appearance of impropriety in all activities." (C JC 2005).

Consider the following scenario. Judge Shipman is presiding over a murder trial and will have to decide the sentencing of a mob boss. The judge made a one-time mistake before becoming a judge and now it has come back to haunt him. The incident is uncovered by the mob and now they are using this to blackmail the judge. How will the judge handle this situation?

If the judge does not do what the mob wants they will expose his secret and his career is over, so the judge believes. If the judge goes along with what the mob wants he would have released a murderer back into society. What is the judge's duty in this case? How will the judge make things right? If the judge wants to do the right thing he will report the crime. This is his only option.

In conclusion, the only option for the judge is to report the blackmail scheme to the authorities because blackmail is a crime and it is the obligation and duty of the judge to report the crime. This would be the right thing to do under the circumstances. The point that there is something in the judge's background should not matter at this point. Additionally, making the decision to report the crime demonstrates a high degree of integrity on the part of the judge. It shows that he is quite capable of applying integrity while performing his duties. Moreover, a judge should always be above reproach. If he succumbs to blackmail it would not stop there, hence resulting in a society overrun with criminals manipulating the justice system for their own personal needs.

FIVE THINKING ERRORS

Overgeneralization – "Taking isolated cases and using them to make wide generalizations". (Burns, 2010.). For example, someone making the statement that one particular race is prone to criminal activity. This is not necessarily true because they are not making the inference on hard data. They are making an assumption. To correct overgeneralization, one might say that for the most part according to data that this particular race the number of criminal activity is high among this particular race.

Mental Filter – "Focusing exclusively on certain, usually negative or upsetting, aspects of something while ignoring the rest." (Burns, 2010.). For example, a person pointing out little negative things about a person and overlooking the positive things about a person. To correct this process focus on the good in a situation instead of the little negative things. For instance, some might see a half of glass of water as half empty but if you look at it in another way the glass is half full.

Jumping to Conclusions – "Assuming something negative where there is actually no evidence to support it." (Burns, 2010.). For example, superstitions. My left eye is twitching this means bad luck. Another example, "assuming the intentions of others." (Burns, 2010). To correct this negative thought process, think positive thoughts. Realize that it is just a superstition.

Emotional Reasoning – "Making decisions and arguments based on how you feel rather than objective reality." (Burns, 2010.). To correct this thought process, say to oneself stop this negative thinking. There is no evidence to support this thought process. To correct this thought process my mother would say, "think with your head and not with your heart". (Holmes, n.d.). Burns says "interrupt anything negative". (Burns, 2010).

Personalization & Blame – "Personalization occurs when you hold yourself personally responsible for an event that isn't entirely under your control." (Burns, 2010). For example, a woman blames herself because she has a miscarriage. Or, consider this, "My neighbors are rude to me, so I must be a bad neighbor." "On the flip side of personalization is blame." (Burns, 2010). The reason why my neighbors are rude to me is because they just do not like me. To correct this problem would be to find out the reasons why and correct the behavior. Or it could just be a misunderstanding or an overgeneralization.

SECTION III

JUVENILES IN THE CRIMINAL JUSTICE SYSTEM

JUVENILE JUSTICE

CHAPTER NINETEEN

JUVENILE JUSTICE AND DELINQUENCY – 19TH CENTURY

According to the Juvenile Crime Statistics report (CSR), "There are currently about seventy million Americans under the age of 18, or a quarter of the total US population. Juvenile crime statistics report that 2.3 million juveniles were arrested in 2002." In addition, "one million juvenile crime cases are processed through the juvenile court system each year and 200,000 are processed through the adult legal system," according to the Juvenile Crime Statistics Report. What does this tell you? These statistics are alarming considering these are considered youths under the age of eighteen. In most cities juveniles are considered to be eighteen or under. Is history repeating itself?

HISTORY TREATMENT OF JUVENILES

In the early 19th Century juveniles who committed crimes were incarcerated and housed in the same facilities as adult offenders. Juveniles were considered to be chattel, "Property" in the eyes of society. Of course this was during a time when there was no juvenile justice system in place. The first juvenile court was established in Chicago in 1899. The juvenile justice system operated successfully for a while until judges would make independent decisions about where to send juvenile offenders, i.e., juvenile facilities or in adult prisons. There was some abuse of the system and policies which resulted in the first major federal legislature (Krisberg 2005).

THE JUVENILE JUSTICE AND DELINQUENCY ACT OF 1974 (P.L. 93-415, 88 STAT. 1109).

"This legislature cultivated and streamlined the content of state policy in the juvenile court system." As stated in an article published on the following site (Miller). The Juvenile Justice and Delinquency Act was made a law as a result of criticism of the juvenile justice system. The Juvenile Justice and Delinquency Act created federal guidelines for the treatment of juvenile offenders. The government also provided funding to states in an effort for them to adhere to the guidelines of the Act.   The philosophy was and is today that juvenile offenders could be rehabilitated and sent back into society as responsible individuals. The consensus was that housing juveniles with adult prisoners would have an adverse effect. "The Act established a system where diversion of juveniles from adult prison would be more successful. Through this system, the states and local governments were provided with grants to help in planning and establishing programs, operating and coordinating programs and evaluating those programs for effectiveness," as per the previous article.

"The emphasis was directed toward education, training research, prevention, diversion, treatment and rehabilitation programs. The programs focus was in the area of juvenile delinquency and improvement to the juvenile justice system." Another turning point in history was in the landmark case of Gerald Gault, 15, who was sentenced to six years in an Arizona youth correction facility for making an obscene telephone call (Krisberg, 2005). Did this call for six years?

LANDMARK 1967 SUPREME COURT DECISION IN RE GAULT

As a result of this case a movement to decriminalize the formal court system and to change juvenile status offenses began. The effort was to determine what was considered a juvenile offense. Just to name a few: truancy, running away, curfew violations, etc., were considered juvenile offenses The movements stressed taking the juveniles out of secured detention centers and training schools to community-based programs that emphasized education and rehabilitation.

MASSACHUSETTS - 1972

In Massachusetts, 1972 the officials "closed all of the state juvenile facilities and literally started over," recruiting Jerome Miller to "clean up a range of scandals and abuses" associated with the previous system (Krisberg, 2005). "Research by Harvard Law School and the National Council on Crime and Delinquency, showed that the Miller reforms successfully reduced the frequency and severity of new offenses of youth in the new programs compared with the training-school graduates." This led to development of similar programs in other states, resulting in Congress establishing the Juvenile and Delinquency Act of 1974 (Krisberg, 2005).

In essence, if we look back at history there are many similarities. Due to rapid crime committed by juveniles the system had to be revamped. If we look at society today, there begins a rapid increase in crime throughout this country of juvenile offenders. If it wasn't for the programs instituted years ago our youths would still be considered chattel.

_____

_____

_____

_____

_____

_____

_____

_____

_____

_____

_____

CHAPTER TWENTY

PARENTS OR PRISON OR ALTERNATIVE

The article by Jennifer Roback Morse, Parents or Prisons, in the Policy Review dated August/September 2003 was indeed well written and researched. However, I felt that I could have appreciated the article more if Morse would have cited research on how to minimize the problem of juvenile delinquency in single family households. There are numerous articles and organizations unbeknownst to quite a few single parents on the reasons for juvenile delinquency and also articles on how we can help to deter juvenile delinquency. In the following pages are just a few articles and websites with information concerning juvenile delinquency which should have been inserted in Morse's article to benefit the public. Other than the absence of positive feedback I thought that Morse's article was very informative and well written and I do agree with her up to a point. It all begins in the home. Education is definitely the key here.

There are many reasons why at risk youths are leading a life of juvenile delinquency. Unbeknownst to most people, I would be the first to admit that there are many alternatives to combating juvenile delinquency.

THE HOME LIFE – CAUSE AND AFFECT

At risk children come from all walks of life, not just the economically deprived. At risks children come from rich, drug addicted, alcoholics, mentally, sexually and psychologically abusive families. For instance, in Morse's article she states that "without parents – two of them, married to each other, working together as a team – a child is more likely to end up in the criminal justice system at some point in his life." Without parents, prison becomes a greater probability in the child's life" (Morse – 2003). This is over generalization.

Statistics would have us to believe that most at risk children come from mostly economically deprived families. This is not necessarily true. The following is an excerpt retrieved from Newsweek published January 13, 2010 about two teenage boys, entitled World's Worst Rotten Rich Kids. The caption reads, Leopold (right) lived in a gabled mansion bought with a shipping fortune, while Loeb's (left) father amassed $10 million as vice president of Sears. But money has its hazards; in this case, distant parents and coldhearted nannies. The teenagers murdered "for the thrill of it," pounding a 14-year-old boy's head in with a chisel in 1924." These juveniles were not economically deprived. Economically deprived juveniles might steal to survive in one way or the other. Juveniles in this day and age learn from their immediate environment, specifically, immediate family, extended family, peers and friends. The solution to the problem of juvenile delinquency is multidimensional (Adams, Arnold, Harmon, Mayabb, Rodriquez and Shirola - 1998). Consequently, the solution would be to address all issues – not just one.

CORRECTING THE PROBLEM

How can we correct the problem? The cause may not be the single parent household however it is one of the causes. Ultimately, the single parent household can be a major issue. If we create a healthy home environment for the family and then we are on our way to decreasing juvenile delinquency. A single parent who falls on bad times and is unable to provide the basic needs of a child, (i.e., food, clothing, housing and recreation, etc.) that child is at risk of becoming a juvenile delinquent. This should be corrected before it gets out of hand. Prison is not the answer for some. Intervention is the answer. There is help. First and foremost, "Parents must begin here because they cannot expect to understand their children unless they have sufficient understanding of themselves" as stated in the article by (Adams, Arnold, Harmon, Mayabb, Rodriquez and Shirola - 1998).

THE CHURCH

The church should be a haven for its members. A church should be a place where members can go for help with problems. There is a saying, "it takes an entire village to raise a child." The authors further states, "Churches can strengthen and improve family life in the direction of delinquency prevention as well as child conservation. It is imperative that they give more attention to the problems and needs of family." (Adams, Arnold, Harmon, Mayabb, Rodriquez and Shirola - 1998).

RECREATIONAL FACILITIES

A very important aspect of a child's life is supervised recreation. Some may take recreation for granted but it is known that if you keep a child involved in recreation they have little time to focus on delinquent acts. "Social reformers in the mid to late 19th century advocated recreation as a means to combat delinquency (Cross, 1990; Larson, 1994; Witt & Crompton, 1997). "Jane Addams, for example, believed that wholesome activities provided by public recreation organizations were "the only agency powerful enough to break into this intensified and unwholesome life" (Addams, 1913, p.24).

Back to Morse's article "Parents or Prisons". Morse states that "The basic self-control and reciprocity that a free society takes for granted do not develop automatically. Conscience development takes place in childhood. Children need to develop empathy so they will care whether they hurt someone or whether they treat others fairly…….." What Morse says is true in a real world. However, in an economically deprived child's world children don't think about this when they are lacking in nourishment or wearing the same clothes to school every day. They are not thinking about this when they are being made fun of in class or in the school yard because of malnutrition.

We must examine the causes of juvenile delinquency - herein lies the problem. Thank you Morse for your very informative article but it does not solve the problem entirely.

THE SOCIAL CONTROL THEORY

What do we mean by Social Control? Some might think manipulation. However, the Social Control Theory in which sociologist gives reference to in our textbook "lies in the strength of an individual's ties to the foundation of society (family, friends, and school)." (p.134). In order to deter youth from committing juvenile criminal acts parents must maintain some social control with their youths. Youth who have close relationships with their families and friends are less likely to commit criminal acts. In addition, youth who have high self-esteem are less likely to commit criminal acts. I would like to add that, "a family that prays together, stays together." If you have close knit family ties then chances of becoming juvenile delinquents are slight. Of course, this could also result in the other way, depending upon the values of the family.

THE LEARNING THEORY

Children learn and imitate quite a bit from their peers. The second picture represents the Learning Theory. It is met to demonstrate that youths can learn criminal behavior by association. If one or two of the youths picture is a juvenile delinquent then just by association the others could adapt to the bad behavior, therefore also becoming juvenile delinquents. There is another saying I would like to quote, "birds of a feather stick together." If we stop and think about it, usually if a person wants to get ahead in life he or she would associate with individuals with the same values. If your self-esteem is low a person would probably associate with others who also have a low self-esteem, thereby increasing chances of bad behavior. (p.129).

CHAPTER TWENTY-ONE

JUVENILE JUSTICE

OFFENSE

An offense relating to the juvenile justice system process is defined as any juvenile behavior prohibited by juvenile law in a particular state. One being, a status offense which is an offense that would not be considered a crime if committed by an adult, i.e. running away from home, truancy, violating curfew, purchasing alcohol or purchasing tobacco. Another offense would be any act committed by a juvenile that would be considered a crime if committed by an adult, i.e. murder, robbery, assault or burglary, etc. If a juvenile is detained for any of the above, the next step would be the Intake.

INTAKE

Intake is the procedure utilized by the juvenile court staff to determine whether to process the case further in court, i.e., bringing formal charges or no action taken against the juvenile or diversion. If it is decided that it would be in the best interest of the juvenile to be removed from the juvenile justice process the diversion procedure would provide the juvenile with treatment services. The juvenile would be given a choice of community service, which is a sanction requiring a juvenile offender to perform a predetermined number of hours of volunteer work, such as cutting grass in public parks or buildings, etc. Another alternative would be counseling and another would be restitution to victims, which is a sanction by which a juvenile offender pays the victim for the harm done and yet another would be to participate in academic programs at his or her school.   If the above-mentioned sanctions were not to be the case then the next step in the juvenile justice system process would be the detention hearing.

DETENTION HEARING

At this point a hearing held in juvenile court during which the judge decides whether the current detention of the juvenile is justified and whether continued detention is warranted. If the juvenile is to continue through the system it is decided whether the juvenile will be released until the hearing into the custody of his or her parents or a responsible adult. "If a juvenile is detained, every state requires that a detention hearing be held within 24 to 72 hours of detention". (p.259). If it is decided to continue detention then the juvenile is detained at a detention center. However for the most part "approximately 50 percent" of all detained juveniles are released after the detention hearing. (p.259). Another decision can also be reached at the detention hearing, i.e., it could be decided whether the hearing should be transferred or whether the case should be transferred to adult court. The next step in the process according to the juvenile justice system flowchart is the preliminary hearing.

PRELIMINARY HEARING

"It is at this point the juvenile can own up to his or her offense by plea bargaining in exchange for concessions made by the prosecutor." (p.263). If the juvenile does not decide to plea bargain the next step in the system would be an adjudication hearing.

ADJUDICATORY HEARING

This hearing is to determine whether there is evidence beyond a reasonable doubt to support the allegations against the juvenile. At this point the juvenile can be found not guilty of the offense by the juvenile court judge, or found to have committed the offense in which he or she have been accused. If the juvenile was found guilty, the next step in the process would be the disposition hearing.

DISPOSITIONAL HEARING

This hearing is held after a juvenile has been adjudicated delinquent to determine what sanction should be imposed on the juvenile, whether the juvenile will receive probation supervision, residential and non-residential or a juvenile correctional facility. If the judge decides that it would be in the best interest of the juvenile and/or the community to receive probation then the juvenile will receive supervisory probation in which he or she would have to report to a probation officer for a specified period of time. "The most common disposition in juvenile court is probation. Probation allows a juvenile to remain in the community as long as he or she abides by certain conditions of probation." (p.13). If the juvenile abides by the rules of probation in the specified period of time, no further action will be taken, however if he or she does not abide then he or she would be placed in a residential or non-residential facility, which would be a camp, ranch or group home, etc. The residential and non-residential sanction imposed would be that the juvenile would be ordered to stay at a supervised residential or non-residential facility for a specified time.

The other alternative for a juvenile offender, if found guilty, would spend time in a correctional facility for a specified length of time. Of course, this would depend on the seriousness of the offense.

GANG INTERVENTION PROGRAM

"According to the National Youth Gang Survey, there are over 27,000 youth gangs and 788,000 youth gang members." (p.402). How are we controlling juvenile gang activity? Law enforcement, prosecution and legislature are using strong arm tactics in attempting to control gang activity. Law enforcement agencies are utilizing such things as "sweeps, surveillance, aggressive patrol, intelligence gathering and follow-up investigation," to control gang activity. (p.402). The above-mentioned tools may help somewhat, but it doesn't scratch the surface of the problem. What needs to be addressed is the reason for the juvenile gangs and why they exist in the first place. The answer is with intervention programs that seek to reduce the criminal activities of gangs by coaxing youth away from gangs and reducing criminality among gang members. I chose to write about an alternative program called, "Homeboy Industries."

HISTORY

The Homeboy Industries started in 1988 in Los Angeles, California as a job training program. It began in the Dolores Mission Parish in Boyle Heights. The person who started the program was Pastor Greg Boyle, S.J. In 1992 Pastor Boyle converted an abandoned warehouse into the first business and it was called Homeboy Bakery. In 2001, Homeboy Industries became a non-profit. In October 2007, Homeboy Industries opened a new $8.5 million headquarters at the Fran and Ray Stark building, in a gang-neutral downtown location. In 2010, Learning Works became a reality, as the new high school with 35 students. (http://www.homeboy-industries.or/employment-services.php).

MISSION AND GOALS OF THE PROGRAM

Pastor Boyle's mission and goals were to, "offer an alternative to gang life for at-risk youth, who were living in the area with the highest concentration of gang activity in the country." Pastor Boyle thought that one of the reasons for juvenile gang affiliation was the cause of the poverty in the economically deprived neighborhoods. So as an alternative to gang affiliation Pastor Boyle's idea of teaching these juveniles a trade was the goal of Homeboy Industries. (http://www.homeboy-industries.org/employment-services.php).

Pastor Boyle approached business owners to agree to hire recovering gang members as employees. The ideal grew to the extent that he acquired an abandoned warehouse and converted it into the first business, Homeboy Bakery." In addition to jobs, Homeboy Industries offers curriculum on anger management, domestic violence, yoga and the list goes on. (http://www.homeboy-industries.org/employment-services.php).

HOMEBOY INDUSTRIES SUCCESS

"In only a few years, Homeboy Industries has had an important impact on the Los Angeles gang problem." (http://www.ncjrs.gov). The program was so successful there was over half of the region's 1,100 known gangs seeking a way out of gang life through Homeboy Industries. Homeboy Industries has since grown to become a national model. Homeboy Industries is celebrating its 22nd anniversary this year and is still fighting the battle against eliminating juvenile gangs. "Homeboy serves as a beacon of hope and opportunity for those seeking to leave gang life, for whom the barriers and challenges are great, and for whom there is virtually no other avenue to enter the mainstream." (http://www.ncjrs.gov).

Father Boyle's mission was to get the juvenile gang members interested in making an honest day living so that this would encourage them to leave the gang life and walk the straight and narrow. This is being accomplished day by day.

JUVENILE JUSTICE SYSTEM OF THE FUTURE

When I think of the future of the juvenile justice system I have to keep in mind why the juvenile justice system was created initially. In 1899 the first juvenile justice system was created in Cook County, Illinois so that juveniles would no longer be treated the same as adults. The first and foremost goal of the juvenile justice system was rehabilitation of juveniles. It was said that juveniles were "less mature than adults, incapable of the same level of intent as adults, and more easily rehabilitated." (p. 4). What has changed?

JUVENILES OF TODAY

Juveniles throughout history became delinquents for various reasons sometimes through no fault of their own. Some became delinquent because of their economic conditions being thrust upon them at a young age. Let us talk about our society and how it contributes to juvenile delinquency. Consider the following. "Adolescents and teens that are raised in lower and working class families are exposed to the dynamics of financial stress on a household." (www.helium.com). In addition, "in order to cope with realities of absolute and relative poverty, a teen may begin stealing for the things he or she needs or desires." (www.helium.com).

The juveniles of today "under this category drop out of school to help support their families and some resort to earning money in illegitimate ways such as selling controlled substances". (www.helium.com). Juveniles of today are angry, malnourished, are insecure and deprived of their rights to grow in healthy environments. The youths of today are drug addicted youths who believes that drugs will help them to cope with their unwanted situations.

As a result, "Young people who persistently abuse substances often experience an array of problems, including academic difficulties, health-related problems (including mental health), poor peer relationships, and involvement with the juvenile justice system. Additionally, there are consequences for family members, the community, and the entire society." (http://www.ojjdp.ncjrs.gov/PUBS/drugid/ration-03.html).

CHALLENGES FOR THE JUVENILE JUSTICE SYSTEM

What are the challenges of the juvenile justice system? The juvenile justice system face many challenges as it attempts to help the fight against juvenile delinquency. But it is not their fight alone. The most dynamic challenge for the juvenile justice system is working simultaneously with the public in combating this problem of juvenile delinquency. Going forward, the juvenile justice system must continue to implement as many programs as possible in order to prevent recidivism of juvenile offenders once they enter the system. The juvenile justice system must continue to actively work in conjunction with the community at large to prevent at-risk children from entering the system. Prevention is the key!

"Most juvenile justice agencies have intervention officers or counselors. These individuals assist troubled youths in finding appropriate programs for intervention." (p.451). In addition, the intervention officers can work in conjunction with teachers and counselors in schools located in high juvenile crime areas in order to identify at-risk youths.

OBJECTIVES

We must understand that in order for the system to operate efficiently the system must be evaluated periodically by monitoring the trends of juvenile delinquency across the country, i.e., when is juvenile delinquency most prevalent? The system must change with the trends.

Is juvenile delinquency more prevalent during the summer months? If so, then we need to look at programs that will keep at-risk youths off the streets and involved in constructive activities. We need to observe the economic conditions of society. Observe what is going on in our immediate communities. Do we have many families out of work? Are there many vacant houses in our neighborhoods? Are there many foreclosures in the neighborhoods? We can no longer bury our heads in the sand. We need to conduct research as to the families who have lost jobs recently. If we have these types of families with children in our communities, then we know there are at-risk youths in our neighborhoods. If so, what can the juvenile justice system and the communities do to help? These are the questions we should be asking.

The development of seminars under the auspices of the juvenile justice system is crucial in educating the public regarding programs available to troubled youths. This will help to prevent juvenile delinquency, especially if the seminars are based on the needs of at-risk youths, i.e., gang affiliations, drug addiction, teenage pregnancy, problem solving skills, social conflict resolution and poverty, just to mention a few. (www. at-risk.com).

More in-depth counseling services provided by law enforcement agencies as well as schools with the help of the juvenile justice system is needed. The juvenile justice system can provide this type of information to the public at large through town meetings as well as seminars developed to help parents cope with at-risk youths. Through these various town meetings a liaison from the juvenile justice system could spearhead the program and can assist parents in recognizing the signs of at-risk youths.

In essence I believe that concentrated efforts should be made regarding prevention of juvenile delinquency prior to reaching the juvenile justice system. We all need to take a long hard look at our state of affairs and know that the responsibility of juvenile delinquency falls on the shoulders of every human being.

The family can play a vital role in preventing juvenile delinquency or can cause juvenile delinquency. But, just imagine not having enough to eat. Imagine going to school on an empty stomach and the child is expected to perform to the best of his or her abilities. How do you think you would feel? Children need nourishment to perform in school. A young child doesn't understand why there is no food for breakfast. We, as a people must remember that the youths of today are our future and responsibility.

Finally, as we face the future, we as a society should keep these issues and objectives foremost in our minds and continue to work closely with the juvenile justice system in solving the problems of juvenile delinquency and reducing recidivism. Our youths run the risk of being stigmatized and identified as recidivists for life. If we don't follow through on the above objectives we also run the risk of perpetuating the cycle.

PROGRAM ENHANCEMENT

The Department of Community Service of Delaware County/Community Corrections was organized to carry out the orders of the Court of Common Pleas, which provides community services to the County by utilizing first and second time offenders as inexpensive labor. Last year I had the opportunity to interview a twelve year old second time offender who I called Jeremy. Jeremy was sentenced to several hours of community service for truancy and other related offenses. I also did a brief interview with the director of the program in which I was not at all impressed with the information I received. It is important to note that the community should be involved and stay involved with the rehabilitation of our troubled youths, not just utilize them as cheap labor. The Department of Community Service under the direction of Walter R. Omlor, Jr. who works in conjunction with the Delaware County Court of Common Pleas to enforce the punishment of the Courts issued to juvenile offenders. What is really the purpose of this program, cheap labor or rehabilitation?

"In an effort to develop a more holistic approach to delinquency prevention, many jurisdictions attempt to move beyond the criminal or juvenile justice system alone and involve more community groups and organizations." (p.160). This excerpt is cited from the chapter on community based groups and organizations as ways and means of dealing with juvenile delinquency.

During my interview with Omlor, I asked if there was any follow-up with the offenders after leaving the program? His answer was "No!" I asked, "How do you keep track of an offender's progress?" "We don't!" Now, is this a program worthy of enhancement? How does this help a juvenile offender? I asked Omlor if he has seen repeat offenders come through the Program. His reply was, "I only know offenders by their identification numbers." Yet, Jeremy was a second time offender. It sounds pretty cold and uncaring. The department's responsibility was to just supervise the offenders in their labor duties.

BUSINESS ONLY!

To this end, I knew that the Program needed enhancement. I found the Program to be only about the business of enforcing the sentencing handed down by the Court and by providing cheap labor service to the County. The individuals who supervise these offenders are not teachers, counselors or professionals of any kind. They are only there to supervise and to make sure the job gets done. The Program is met to be a punishment, not to rehabilitate. The Program is not based on rehabilitation but "to provide community service workers at various public buildings, youth facilities and firehouses, public and parochial schools to perform various duties utilizing these first and second time offenders" (www.co.de.aware.pa.us).

ELIMINATE THIS CONCEPT - REDUCING OVERCROWDING IN PRISONS

Omlor explained that the reason for establishing Community Corrections was to "reduce prison overcrowding and provide invaluable resources of labor for community improvement projects." (www.co.de. aware.pa.us). In support of community based organizations, most are assets to the communities throughout the country. Community based organizations first and foremost should have the rehabilitation of juvenile offenders in mind, not for eliminating overcrowding in prisons. The mission of the Delaware County Department of Community Service/Community Corrections mission statement needs to be revisited and the concept should be changed so that it addresses rehabilitation of juvenile offenders.

SEPARATION OF JUVENILE AND ADULT OFFENDERS NEEDED

In essence, the changes that should be made are that first and second time offenders should be taught and shown how the seriousness of their actions not only affects their lives but how their actions affect the lives of their family and friends. During my interview with Omlor, there was no role playing or classroom activities or counseling involved. These offenders need to know that they matter and can make a difference in society and that they are not just a file number. Because of the concept of the Program, it not only has juvenile offenders it also consists of adult first and second time offenders as well. The adult offenders should be separated from the juvenile offenders.

PARTICIPATION IN CLASSES

Going forward, as the juvenile offenders perform their community service hours they should also be required to participate in various classes, such as counseling, educational, anger management and problem solving classes. Most importantly, it is very important that there should be incorporated into the Program a follow through process to monitor the progress of each offender to eliminate recidivism.

FOLLOW-UP NEEDED

Presently, a follow-up system is not in place and I reiterate it should be a priority for reinforcement of what was learned. I don't know what happened to Jeremy. But at the end of our interview he promised me that this was his last time through the system. How can you be so sure? I asked. "I am responsible for my actions," he said. (Juvenile Interview – Jeremy. May, 2010). I will follow up on Jeremy.

_____

_____

_____

_____

_____

_____

_____

_____

_____

_____

CHAPTER TWENTY-THREE

THEORY IMAGE

THE SOCIAL CONTROL THEORY

What do we mean by Social Control? Some might think manipulation. However, the Social Control Theory in which sociologist gives reference to in our textbook "lies in the strength of an individual's ties to the foundation of society (family, friends, and school)." (p.134). In order to deter youth from committing juvenile criminal acts parents must maintain some social control with their youths. Youth who have close relationships with their families and friends are less likely to commit criminal acts. In addition, youth who have high self-esteem are less likely to commit criminal acts. I would like to add that, "a family that prays together, stays together." If you have close knit family ties then the chances of becoming juvenile delinquents are slight. Of course, this could also result in the other way, depending upon the values of the family.

THE LEARNING THEORY

Children learn and imitate quite a bit from their peers. The second picture represents the Learning Theory. It is met to demonstrate that youths can learn criminal behavior by association. If one or two of the youths picture is a juvenile delinquent then just by association the others could adapt to the bad behavior, therefore also becoming juvenile delinquents. There is another saying I would like to quote, "birds of a feather flock together." If we stop and think about it, usually if a person wants to get ahead in life he or she would associate with individuals with the same values. If your self-esteem is low a person would probably associate with others who also have a low self-esteem, thereby increasing chances of bad behavior. (p.129).

WHAT IS THE PURPOSE OF THE JUVENILE JUSTICE SYSTEM?

_____

_____

_____

_____

_____

_____

_____

_____

_____

THE OUTCOME – THE JUVENILE JUSTICE SYSTEM, COMMUNITY, FAMILY – ALL WORKING HAND IN HAND

_____

_____

_____

_____

_____

_____

_____

_____

_____

SECTION IV

SOCIETY, LAW AND THE GOVERNMENT

POLICE TECHNOLOGY/COMMUNICATION SYSTEMS

LICENSE PLATE CAMERA SYSTEMS

According to an article published on the website of Surveillance Video.com, (a site that markets and sells surveillance systems) states that a "License Plate Camera System is a surveillance system used primarily by law enforcement" that records license plate numbers of moving vehicles, especially those running red lights. The system takes pictures of the license plate numbers resulting in tickets being mailed out to the registered address on file. In the event of a dispute in traffic court the pictures from the camera can be used as evidence of the traffic violation. This system is hooked up to a database where information can be obtained on the vehicle's owner i.e., an address or name of the owner of the vehicle. (http://www.surveillance-video.com).

"There is another version of the license plate camera which is hooked up to a DVR and the surveillance footage is thereby recorded for review," as explained in the article. "This version is utilized by homeowners and gated communities to keep track of who enters and exits their neighborhood. It is an effective deterrent of potential crime in this way". "It becomes not only effective but an affordable deterrent with the difference in cost". (http://www.surveillance-video.com).

SECURITY CAMERA SYSTEM

The website mentioned earlier has been in business for thirty-five (35) years and has been selling security systems to the public and law enforcement professionals. The above-mentioned security camera system is just another one of the systems sold and marketed by Surveillance—video.com. According to the article, the security camera system can be utilized in homes, schools, businesses, correctional institutions, in courts and law enforcement. This system can easily be installed and it monitors the activities of businesses. If it is installed in the home it will monitor the activities of the home. You can arrange for a motion detector to alert the owner via pager or e-mail when there is a disturbance at a home or business and law enforcement can be notified at once. (http://www.surveillance-video.com/comsys.htm1)

POLICE OBSERVATION DEVICES (POD)

I mentioned the Police Observation Devices (POD) in an earlier paper. I believe that it is important to reiterate the importance of the POD because it was so successful in combating crime in Chicago for the Chicago Police Department. PODs are fantastic because they are placed in high crime areas to deter criminals. PODs are a second set of eyes for the police. "The POD camera system was utilized to monitor the area for suspicious activity," according to an article entitled "POD Success Stories". PODs are definitely useful in law enforcement and in court. The reason being, a person committing a crime is caught on camera. This could be utilized for evidence in court. PODs are also used for "reverse stings, we can not only watch crime conditions, but we can also keep an eye on our officer's safety," explained Sergeant Gina Dwyer of the Chicago Police Department. I believe the Police Observation Devices market themselves. They are located where they can be seen by criminals and citizens. I am sure that they are marketed on the Internet as well. (https://portal.chicagopolice.org).

In conclusion the communication systems mentioned above would be instrumental in law enforcement, corrections and the courts. For the most part they are attainable commercially. The importance of the above systems is that they can be purchased online for professional and private use.

_____

_____

_____

_____

_____

HOW TO ELIMINATE FIRST TIME JUVENILE OFFENDERS

Juveniles are going through the criminal justice system at alarming rates. "In 1999 there were 2.5 million arrests of persons under the age of 18. Twenty-seven (27%) percent of the arrests involved females and thirty-two (32%) were youths under 15." (Siegel & Senna, 1997, p.10). Why? What can be done to minimize the number? Let us begin by focusing on the Why. Then we can focus on the what. We want to look at the technology utilized by law enforcement in the prevention of crime relating to juveniles entering the criminal justice system.

_____

_____

_____

_____

_____

_____

_____

CHAPTER TWENTY-EIGHT

RECREATION AS A DETERRENCE OF JUVENILE CRIME

Growing up in a dysfunctional family is one reason why juveniles are going astray. What can be done? Research is being conducted concerning recreation playing a major role in combating juvenile crime. An Article written by Wayne W. Munson suggests that "certain types of recreation activities promote conventional values and prevent delinquency by impacting youths' bonds of beliefs." (Hirschi, 1969; Siegel & Senna, 1997).

The following excerpt is an article found on the internet entitled, "Recreation and Juvenile delinquency prevention: how recreation professionals can design programs that really work- Research Update".

Landers and Landers (1978) did some investigation on the effects of participation in extracurricular activities on juvenile delinquency. The study consisted of data of 521 students from a northeastern high school, which were grouped in different activity categories and both or neither category. After composing the list it was taken to the town courthouse to determine the number of misdemeanor or felony offenses of students in each category.

The results indicated a significant association between delinquency and extracurricular activity participation. The participants who didn't participate in an activity were more likely to engage in delinquent acts and those who were on the activity lists were less likely to engage in delinquent acts. (Munson, 2002).

_____

_____

_____

CHAPTER TWENTY-NINE

HOW THE GOVERNMENT AND LAW ENFORCEMENT CAN HELP

Giving reference to an article written by Robert O. Heck, he mentions a bill entitled, Violent Youth Predator Act of 1996 (H.R. 3565), sponsored by Representative Bill McCollum (R-FL). This bill will provide block grants to Local and State officials to help combat violent juvenile crime. How would this help? Heck points out that the States police forces would be utilized more effectively, "by integrating innovative community police work with the efforts of community leaders and other agencies in the criminal justice system." (Wootton & Heck, 2010). Going forward, let's look at Cognitive Behavior Therapy.

COGNITIVE BEHAVIORAL THERAPY

CAN HELP PREVENT JUVENILE CRIME

Patrick Clark has written an article entitled, "Preventing Future Crime with Cognitive Behavior Therapy.   Clark cites a study performed by Mark Lipsey of Vanderbilt University, which Lipsey examined the effectiveness of young offenders by analyzing 548 studies. "The therapy assumes that most people can become conscious of their own thoughts and behaviors and then make positive changes to them." After grouping the evaluations into categories he found that the effects of the interventions were that those based on punishment and deterrence appeared to increase criminal recidivism. However those based on the therapeutic approach, counseling, skill building and multiple services had the greatest impact in reducing further criminal behavior. (Wootton & Heck, 2010).

In conclusion, community based policing, recreation and cognitive behavior therapy is just a few methods being utilized in reducing criminal recidivism among juvenile offenders. The above-referenced programs are good programs and have proven successful in places like New York and Charleston, South Carolina.

I like to conclude this paper with a quote from an unknown individual. "It takes a community to raise a child". If we remember this we have a chance to save one child at a time.

POLICE SURVEILLANCE CAMERAS

If I was the chief executive of a law enforcement agency I would want to pursue getting funding for police surveillance cameras for high crime areas in the community. I believe that the crime statistics would be lower as a result.   It would help the citizens of the community to feel safer in their homes and increase community policing. For example, if a person who lives in the community observes a crime he or she can call the police station to report the crime and location.

INCREASE IN EFFICIENCY

Investing in surveillance cameras will help to focus more on high crime areas. The response time would be faster, aide in controlling curfew in the community and instrumental in helping to eliminate first time offenders. PODs were introduced in the Chicago Police Department in 2003 in an effort to control crime in the high crime areas of the city. (https://portal.chicagopolice.org).

EFFECTIVENESS OF LAW ENFORCEMENT

PODs would give the police another set of eyes to watch the neighborhoods. It would cut down on the time in responding to crime because the police monitoring the neighborhoods could focus in on the crime immediately and dispatch a car to the place in question. PODs have been proven to lower the statistics in the high crime areas in Chicago so much they have extended the areas PODs are utilized.

Police Observance Devices would be asset in any police department where they experience high crime areas. It would be instrumental in preventing drug trafficking in areas where police have problems policing. Overall, the devices will eventually have a positive effect on the entire community. Eventually, the high crime areas would be lower crime areas.

CORRELATIONAL RESEARCH

Jessica, a homeowner observes around tax season her neighbors would make major home repairs and spends money on large ticket items. Jessica's theory is they receive their refund checks from Internal Revenue Service (IRS), which she believes is the reason for the purchases.

THEORY

Supposedly, the definition of a theory is, "an organized system of ideas that seeks to explain why two or more events are related." (McGraw-Hill, 2009). To prove her theory she decided to conduct a correlational research study. In Chapter 2 of the text the definition of correlational research is, "Research designed to examine the nature of the relationship between two or more naturally occurring variables.

Is Jessica's theory correct? How can Jessica prove the validity of her theory? Did the correlation of the receipt of refund checks received from IRS around tax season motivate her neighbors to make home improvements and other purchases around tax season.

HYPOTHESIS

According to Chapter 2 of the Publication of the Fifth Edition of Social Psychology (2009) a "Hypothesis is an educated guess or prediction about the nature of things based upon a theory" (McGraw-Hill, 2009).

OBTAINING APPROVAL TO CONDUCT SURVEY

Jessica decides to get permission from her neighbors to conduct a scientific study to prove her theory. The scientific method she is utilizing is correlational research with the use of surveys. The goal of correlational research "is to find out whether one or more variables can predict other variables." However, "correlational research allows us to find out what variables may be related". Again, "the fact that two things are related or correlated does not mean there is a causal relationship. Two things can be correlated without there being a causal relationship." See website: (http://www.psychologyandsociety.com/correlationalstudy.html.)

COLLECTION OF DATA

Jessica decides to go door to door taking surveys. Jessica surveys a total of 100 neighbors of 150 to insure validity and thoroughness. For example, the following are sample closed and open end questions on the survey: 1) Do you file your tax return early or late during the tax season? 2) If you file your tax return early, why? And 3) what do you spend your refund on? "Surveys and questionnaires are one of the most common methods used in psychological research." See website: (www.sychologyandsociety.com)

ANALYZING THE DATA

Jessica gathers data and reports the results. "The primary benefit of conducting correlational research is prediction. This method allows researchers to predict a change in one variable by knowing the value of another variable." (McGraw-Hill, 2009). Simply put, will the value of receiving the refund from IRS motivate participants to spend their money on home improvement?

In conclusion, the survey method is fast, inexpensive and very easy to conduct. Large amounts of data can be collected in a relatively short period of time. Surveys are also considered to be more flexible; however, the survey method has its disadvantages because the survey questions might not be precise enough or the researcher might not have a representative sample in order to get results. Subsequently, another variable may enter that interferes with the outcome of the study. For instance, participants may put the refund in a savings account. Or, participants may not be completely forthright (Cherry, 2010).

GROUP DYNAMICS

Three years ago I accepted a volunteer position as Director of a small library in the community in which I live. Our small community is divided into south and north. The library was in its infancy stage and needed a lot of work. It was not staffed so the need for a library staff was needed. I thought this would be an excellent example of group dynamics. I cannot give you all the details but I will give you some of the highlights. The temporal model of group membership according to Richard Moreland and John Levine involves five phases, which demonstrates how individuals are changed by group membership and how groups are changed by the individual's ideas and actions, etc. (Moreland and Levine, 1982).

INVESTIGATION PHASE - PROSPECTIVE MEMBER

During the investigation phase I was interviewed for the position, made an offer and I accepted the volunteer position. The library as I mentioned above was in its infancy stage and in much disarray. The interview itself took place in the library among borrowed books. The need for organization was apparent. I knew that a director was certainly needed to organize the library. I found that this would be a major challenge. I was not intimidated by the job because I had successfully organized another library. The need and desire for successfully organizing this library would benefit me as well as my community. (Cini et al., 1993)

SOCIALIZATION PHASE - NEW MEMBER

The first thing I had to do was to obtain other volunteers. I was introduced to the working board members. The job of the working board was to oversee as well as work in the library. They explained the rules, policies and politics of the township. Organizing a township library was one of my personal goals. At first the job was rewarding but then it became to be a burden. I started to run into obstacles that should have been easy to overcome, but to the contrary.

MAINTENANCE PHASE- FULL MEMBER

All duties and responsibilities were not revealed initially. For instance, I had to be responsible for fundraising. I became disenchanted with the project. My attitude toward my job began to change. The group's attitude began to change. However we all continued to work hard. The library was up and running, books were catalogued, I was purchasing new books and the library was being utilized by the community. It was not always utilized in a positive way. (Franzoi, p. 302)

RESOCIALIZATION PHASE - MARGINAL MEMBER

The youths that would frequent the library became very unruly and disrespectful. It was during this phase, (the third year) the board attempted to convince me that things would change. The disrespect of the youths was my breaking point, especially since this was on a volunteer basis. There was nothing more that I could give to the community, so I resigned.

REMEMBRANCE PHASE - EX-MEMBER

My presence at the library changed the community as well as the volunteer staff. However I learned that people don't always appreciate your efforts. For the past year I registered my concerns about the youths, but my concerns fell on death ears. I am sorry to say, the library is no longer operational. My biggest concern when I was contemplating resigning was that the library probably would close if I was to leave. The library is now just a little white building sitting alone with no one to care for it. In my community it's all about politics. By the way the community is basically African American. Need I say more? (Franzoi, p.303)

THE CASE OF GLEN

This single male has low self-esteem and has a negative self-image. He is the victim of classical conditioning as a result of the award system during his childhood. Glen was not allowed to show any type of emotion as a child, therefore unable to grow into who he really is as a person. This caused Glen to become a victim of deindividuation. His defining moment was when his boss had a heart attack and left Glen in charge of the store. Despite his low self-esteem and loss of individual identity, Glen has the potential for a good manager, so his boss thought. Unfortunately, because of the classical conditioning and the loss of his individuality, Glen shows a lack of confidence.

In addition to the above, Glen also exhibits attachment issues. Attachment is defined as the strong emotional bond that develops between an infant his or her caretaker. Unfortunately, in Glen's case he still has those attachments with his mother. For example, the keepsake from his mother in which she made for him when he was three years old – he still has it. His father also played a significant role in Glen's early childhood and his behavior as an adult. Glen has a deep rooted problem with having to be in control all the time and bottling up his emotions. This is due to his father rewarding him each time he successfully stayed in control of his emotions when in a stressful situation. This also is a prime example of the classical conditioning he experienced during adolescent and early adulthood.

His lack of confidence is due to how he feels about himself and his performance on the job. He feels that he cannot perform to the best of his ability and he seems to be experiencing the hindsight bias by predicting the outcome of his situation by stating that because he feels that he may lose his job for poor performance. The definition of the hindsight bias is "the tendency, once an event has occurred, to overestimate our ability to have foreseen the outcome". Glen is assuming that the store will not meet its sales goals and that he will never make his sales goals in the future.

Moreover, Glen's breakup with his girlfriend of three years further demonstrates his lack of confidence, low self-esteem and his hindsight biases. After the traumatic experience of the breakup he now feels that he will never find another relationship and he will never marry. Glen also has intimacy issues associated with the breakup of his girlfriend. As a result of his previous relationship, Glen is experiencing the fearful-avoidant attachment style, whereas the text defines as "an expectation about social relationship characterized by low trust and avoidance of intimacy, combined with a feeling of being unworthy of others' love and a fear of rejection."

Finally, Glen experiences high anxiety when he has to speak in front of an audience, i.e., the company's regional meeting, demonstrating his fear of public speaking. The amygdala which is the part of the brain that is associated with emotional responses and the brain's alarm system for threat, pain and danger. Glen's fear for public speaking causes his alarm to go off, hence the sweating and the high heart rate. Another important factor is that Glen is an introvert. Individuals who are introverted normally dislike speaking in front of groups. They are not comfortable in that type of situation just because of the arousal in that area of the brain. Introverts, such as Glen, avoid social interaction or situations such as public speaking so that they can maintain control.

In essence Glen's attitude about himself, his self-awareness, low self-esteem and his lack of an intimate relationship is the result of his classical conditioning from his false sense of attachment with his parents. As a result his upbringing has influenced his behavior as an adult leaving him very confused. In Glen's case all the above-mentioned concepts are related to each other because simply its speaks to the behavior of Glen and his social problems.

_____

_____

_____

_____

_____

_____

_____

_____

_____

CHAPTER THIRTY

<u>JOURNAL ENTRY</u>

THOUGHTS ON INTEGRITY AND HOW IT PLAYS A PART IN OUR EVERYDAY LIVES AND IT'S EFFECT ON A CHILD'S PERSONALITY.

I must say that the most meaningful concept for me is in Chapter 7, Social Influence, page 267 entitled, "The Minority Can Influence the Majority". History dictates the importance of the phrase, "The minority can influence the majority." Reflect on Martin Luther King, Jr. and what he did for all people, he was a trailblazer. Reflect on John F. Kennedy, Jr., and think about what he did for the civil rights movement. Reflect upon Rosa Parks and that famous bus ride that involved into a national protest against inequality. Jackie Robinson, one man, broke the color barrier in baseball. Stop and think about, did you ever think that day would come when we would have a black President. Barack Obama has given hope to millions.

If we understand for whence we come we can understand where we are going. The above-mentioned concept means so very much to me because it reaffirms my beliefs that just one person can make a difference. All we need to do is stand our ground and fight for what is right. As I mentioned previously, I have been subjected to prejudice and discrimination on my job. Most people would say if you don't like it there, leave. That is not an option for me. I am determined I will not allow their attitudes to change my life. I am determined that in my place of employment the discrimination and prejudice stops with me. And, it is slowly happening. I know that I am making a difference.www.biography.com/blackhistory

CHAPTER THIRTY-ONE

WORLD VIEW

It was 1957 when I first encountered prejudice and racism. I was only thirteen years of age when my family and siblings moved from North Philadelphia to West Oak Lane, the first black family to break the color barrier on this tree lined block. Needless to say our new neighbors were not pleased. Almost immediately our neighbors went door to door complaining because we moved into their neighborhood. Soon, thereafter it was an exodus of families moving out of their homes because we moved into the neighborhood. This is a perfect example of the self-fulfilling prophecy explained by Robert Merton in 1948. "Merton introduced the concept of the self-fulfilling prophecy to describe how others' expectations about a person, group, or situation can actually lead to fulfillment of those expectations." (Merton, p.8)

Simply stated, what others perception of you will be communicated through their thoughts and actions leading the receiver of the message eventually leading the individual or group to the self-fulfilling prophecy. The exodus was an awakening to me of prejudice and racism in action. Of course, I didn't understand it then but I do now. Prejudices and racism are learned behaviors. It affected me in a negative way then and stayed with me all through junior high and high school.   I, not only, experienced the prejudices in my community but also in school. As a teenager, I was no different than any other, I was confused and introverted. I had mixed feelings as a teenager during those years in junior high school. Moreover, when I reached 8th grade I needed to choose the curriculum I wanted to pursue. All students were to meet with guidance counselors to select the desired curriculum for high school. My counselor's advice to me was, "You are not college material". I was devastated. That advice stayed with me through the rest of junior high and throughout high school and well into adulthood. Perhaps, my counselor thought he was helping me but it was just another form or racism. This again, was a perfect example of the self-fulfilling Prophecy. (Merton p. 8) I developed a serious inferiority complex and found myself afraid to pursue the very things that motivated me. Fortunately, I know now that what one perceives you to be it is not necessarily who you are. Additionally, how our neighbors perceived our family led me to believe that we were inferior beings.

It took me forty years to figure out what I was subjected to in junior high school. This is why I went to

Community College of Philadelphia and why I am at the University today. I needed to change my perception of who I am. I now have an Associate Degree in Journalism and now I am pursuing a Bachelor Degree in Criminal Justice. I no longer have the same goals as before because of my experiences and age. I have since changed my goals to coexist with who I am and what is needed in my community today. It is now my decision, not because someone is telling me I am not capable. Prejudices and racism will always exist but I know what I am facing. The best part of my development is that it has inspired me to examine the reasons why there are prejudices and racism in the world. I am a stronger person now and quite extroverted because of the adversity. I am no longer afraid to fight for my beliefs.

SOCIOLOGY

JENNY RODRIQUEZ, A JUNIOR AT MCTOWN HIGH SCHOOL

After reading the fictional narrative on "Living in McTown", I felt the Jenny Rodriquez family narrative alluded to the social stratification theory. The social stratification theory which includes the caste and class systems concept is the reason why the Jenny Rodriquez family were subjected to the negative treatment received by the town people.

The Rodriquez Family reminded me somewhat of my teenage years when my family relocated to West Oak Lane. Our new neighbors went from door to door discussing their unhappiness about our arrival in the neighborhood. Both my family and my neighbors were experiencing the effects of cultural shock. I know that cultural shock is an uneasy feeling when one experiences an unfamiliar way of life. It is now obvious that they were not used to living in a community with African American people. They were not familiar with our ways or our living habits so they felt uneasy and threatened by our presence in their neighborhood. Yet, we felt the same way. This was new to our family as well. This was what sociologist call cultural change. The neighbors who moved out of the neighborhood were experiencing cultural lag. Those neighbors who continued to live in the neighborhood experienced cultural integration. We all continued to live in peace.

The Rodriquez family however continued to experience cultural shock to the point that Jenny couldn't wait to leave McTown. The social interaction between the Rodriquez family and the town people was very negative to say the least. Social stratification also is evident in how the town's people treated the Rodriquez

Family. It was evident that they felt that they were of a lower caste and not worthy of their friendship or to live amongst their family and friends. One would assume that there was little chance of social mobility in McTown for the Rodriquez family because of the caste system in place in McTown. A caste system is social stratification based on ascription or birth. The Rodriquez family were just farmers and not in the same class according to some in McTown.

Sam Votapka, a Retired Factory Forman

Sam Votapka illustrates Gerhard Lenski's explanation of society and technology. Lenski explains the progression of industry and how it systematically transforms society. He talks about how the need for many workers creates large urban areas where factories were located and ultimately causes social inequality by increasing poverty and how it becomes a social problem. Votapka talks about how McTown was once a thriving farming town and once it became industrialized the farms disappeared and the town began to experience poverty. As a result of deterioration the town began to show signs of structural social mobility. It demonstrates a decisive shift in the social position of large numbers of people due to the change in society. As a result the young adults began to leave and go to the big cities for jobs just like Votapka's daughter, who he encouraged to move to Chicago.

MARY SMITH, A MARRIED WORKING MOTHER OF THREE

Mary Smith demonstrates signs of role conflict. Role conflict is conflict among the roles corresponding to two or more statuses. For example Mary works for an attorney as a paralegal in town but it causes her stress because it's difficult to work and be a good mother to her children and good wife to her husband. For the most part we all occupy many social positions at the same time and Mary is no exception to the rule. A status set is utilized to refer to all the statuses one might hold at any given time. Mary occupies the social position as a wife, mother and employee all at the same time. If we look at role strain one can concur that Mary is also experiencing role strain due to the fact that the demands of her job as a paralegal is conflicting with her obligation of taking care of her children.

TELL ME A JOKE

One fine morning at F.A. O. Schwarz, three-year old Jennifer Berkowitz simply refused to get off the red tricycle she had been riding for close to an hour. Her mother pleaded, and so did the salespeople, but the little girl flew into a rage and would not be budged.

Suddenly, the store manager remembered that he had recently met and chatted with the renowned child psychologist Irving Green. He also remembered that Dr. Green's office was only three blocks from the toy store. The Berkowitz girl was fast becoming impossible, and the manager decided that nothing could be lost by calling Dr. Green. Perhaps he could spare a few minutes to help with this annoying problem? Yes, said Dr. Green, he would be happy to come right over.

There was a collective sigh of relief as the distinguished psychologist marched into the store. Without talking to anybody, he made his way to the girl on the red tricycle, leaned over, smiled, and whispered something in her ear. At once, and without a word of protest, Jennifer jumped off the tricycle as though it were on fire, and ran over to rejoin her mother.

As soon as the girl and her mother had left the store, the sales force crowded around Dr. Green. They were eager to know what words of psychiatric wisdom he had uttered to get the girl off the tricycle.

"Oh, it was nothing, really," said the therapist. "I said to her: "Listen, tzatskelah, if you don't get off that thing right now, I'm gonna give you such a potch on the tuchis that you won't sit down for a week!"

This joke demonstrates that the theoretical analysis of culture, i.e., cultural universals. For instance little Jennifer was being a spoiled little girl, wanting her way. This is a trait in which you would find in any culture. The joke also displays the social conflict theory. Little Jennifer creates a conflict in the store between the store personnel and the parents by her behavior. The store personnel knowing that they cannot express their true feelings concerning the situation, of course this creates inequality.

This joke indicates that little Jennifer was out of control because of lack of discipline. As stated in the text, "the family also has the job of teaching children skills, values, and beliefs. Introducing the distinguished psychologist into the equation brought a sigh of relief for everyone concerned.

Evidently, the psychologist told the little girl if she didn't get off the tricycle he would give her a spanking on her behind that she wouldn't be able to sit down for a week. This seemed to be resocialization on a smaller scale.

CHAPTER THIRTY-TWO

DISCUSSION – APPOINTMENT OF JUDGES BY A U.S. PRESIDENT

In 1989, former President George H. W. Bush, appointed Clarence Thomas as a federal judge to the United States Court of Appeal for the District of Columbia Circuit. On July 1, 1991, George H.W. Bush nominated Thomas to replace Thurgood Marshall, who had recently announced his retirement. Thomas was confirmed on October 15, 1991 with a 52-48 vote. What did Thomas and Bush have in common? They both had similar conservative ideologies, which was definitely influential in Bush's selection.

Clarence Thomas had an opposition to affirmative action and he was not and still not an advocate for civil rights. He is proactive with government having control. George H.W. Bush believed in the stare decisis while he was in office and this is definitely a conservative ideology. According to an article written by Douglas T. Kendall of the Washington Post on October 14, 2004, it seems that Thomas' position on the stare decisis was becoming more liberal than conservative. For your information, "stare decisis" simply means respecting or abiding on cases that have already been decided. There is no room for interpretation.

I would surmise that Bush and Thomas both in the beginning had very similar conservative ideologies. Thomas was a republican when Bush nominated him, as like Bush. So it stands to reason that he would select a person with conservative ideologies as like himself. So, yes I know that Bush's decision was predicated on the fact that Thomas was a republican with conservative ideologies. Presidents usually nominate individuals with similar ideologies.

ELENA KAGAN DISCUSSION

Senate confirmed Solicitor General Elena Kagan as the 112th Justice of the Supreme Court on Thursday with a 63-37 vote carrying the support of 58 democrats and 5 republicans. After research of several websites,

I could not find too many concerns of the media. There was some concerns raised dealing with the "First Amendment "Don't Ask, Don't Tell." In addition, there were concerns about on-campus military recruiting.

In addition to the above, there was also a concern about her idea of having cameras at the Supreme Court. According to Julie Hilden, Kagan's ideal would "pose some risks – for instance, the risk of inadvertently revealing jurors' identities, etc….." (Hilden).

The media in some instances felt that Kagan was invasive in some of her answers, such as, "On the campaign-finance topic, Kagan also refused to "take off the advocate's hat and put on the judge's hat." It was further pointed out, "That stance is troubling, though, for Kagan has never been a judge, and surely we deserve some insight into what kind of judge she will be."

The <u>Associated Press says,</u> "In Nominating Kagan to replace Justice John Paul Stevens, President Barack Obama has Chosen a Brilliant Legal Scholar."

<u>CBS News" Jan Crawford says,</u> "The Justices really like her. You should see Justice Scalia, a conservative and Kagan going back and forth. So the White House sees that as a real plus, and they expect her to be a very effective jurist on that court." This is ironic being that they started a rumor that she might be a lesbian.

Finally, explain if you think the issues discussed were relevant and if not what should the media have been discussing? Did race, class, gender, sexuality, religion come into play and do you think it should have- why/why not?

The issue of race did come up at one point, but was met with humor by Kagan. The race or religion of a nominee of a Supreme Court Justice should not matter.

Unfortunately, there is a rumor that Kagan may be a lesbian. The rumor has not been validated but in my opinion this is a question in which I believe should be asked. I say this because the U.S. Constitution is based on the Bible. In my opinion some things are just wrong.

"Our laws and our institutions must necessarily be based upon and embody the teachings of the Redeemer of mankind. It is impossible that it should be otherwise; and in this sense and to this extent our civilization and our institutions are emphatically Christian." – United States Supreme Court, 1892.

Read: Leviticus 20:13: "If a man lies with a male as with a woman, both of them have committed an abomination; they shall be put to death, their blood is upon them".

JUDICIAL DECISION MAKING ANALYSIS
INTRODUCTION

Brown v. Board of Education, 347 U.S. 483 (1954) was a U.S. Supreme Court decision that will remain in the history of the United States for years to come. This decision overturned the law "Separate but Equal" in the Fourteenth Amendment of the Constitution and replaced it with a unanimous vote saying, "that in the field of public education the doctrine of 'Separate but Equal' has no place in education." (Findlaw, 2010).

The case was argued in the lower courts and was ruled against and was appealed and reargued and denied. Eventually it made it to the United States Supreme Court where a "unanimous vote" decided that the law was unconstitutional. (Findlaw, 2010).

LEGAL SUB-CULTURE

The legal Sub-Culture had some influence in the decision process in the lower courts because of several cases researched but one of importance stood out and that was Plessy v. Ferguson. Plessy v. Ferguson was based on the doctrine "Separate but Equal" meaning the black schools were equal with respect to buildings, curricula, transportation, etc. (Findlaw, 2010). The "Equal Protection Clause" in the Fourteenth Amendment "requires each State to provide equal protection under the law to all people within its jurisdiction". (Findlaw, 2010). Accordingly, meaning African American students should be allowed to attend white public schools.

JUDICIAL BACKGROUND

As for the judicial background, let us take a look at where some of the original cases began. In States such as Kansas - where it all began, South Carolina, Virginia and Delaware, just to name a few, these States are no stranger to discrimination and racism, thereby being in favor of segregation in public schools. Judges are supposed to be neutral, but do you think if there were any African American judges on the bench (Trial or State level) in Brown v. Board of Education, would it have made a difference?

POLITICAL PARTY AFFILIATION

Political Party Affiliation during the time of Brown v. Board of Education did in deed have influence on the outcome of the case in the lower courts. Why? In the lower courts many of the judges were probably recommended by colleagues of similar backgrounds to the bench and were elected by their constituents to the bench or by senators, as well.

PUBLIC OPINION

Public opinion during the time of Brown v. Board of Education did have influence as to the outcome of the case do to the publicity of the trial. This was a high profile case and needed to be resolved fairly and honestly in a timely fashion. It had involvement of many community organizations on behalf of the plaintiffs. One being the National Chapter of the NAACP.

POLITICS

Politics would definitely play a vital role in the outcome of the case because judges depended on their constituents to vote them into the justice system as judges.

Discrimination and racism was the key issue in Brown v. Board of Education. It was unclear as to the interpretation of the Fourteenth Amendment, however the Supreme Court ruled on behalf of the plaintiffs by stating that "Segregation of white and colored children in public schools has a detrimental effect upon the colored children." And, in conclusion, as mentioned earlier "the Separate but Equal" doctrine adopted in Plessy v. Ferguson, has no place in the field of public education." (Findlaw, 2010).

CHAPTER THIRTY-THREE

THE CRIMINAL TRIAL

First, we must understand that the process of the criminal trial varies from state to state, however with similarities. Usually, the first step leading up to a criminal trial is the arrest. The suspect is read his or her "Miranda Rights". (This is very important because a suspect can escape prosecution on a technicality, if he or she is not read their rights).

The Arrest: There are two basic types of arrest. An arrest **"with a warrant"** issued after a complaint has been made by another person and approved by a judge if the judge thinks there is   probable cause for the arrest. An arrest **"without a warrant"** if a crime is committed in front of an officer, it is justifiable for arrest or if the police officer believes there is probable cause for an arrest.

The next step in the process is the **"First Appearance"**. After the suspect is arrested he or she is booked, fingerprinted, photographed, records are checked to see if there are any outstanding warrants or if the suspect has any prior offenses on his or her record. The facts of the case are recorded for future reference. The suspect then appears in front of a magistrate or lower level judge within twenty-four hours or within forty-eight hours if arrested without a warrant, this varies from state to state. The suspect is informed of the charges and then once again the suspect is informed of his or her Miranda Rights; which are as follows. Right to remain silence…..etc. Right of an attorney….and etc. Right to a speedy trial…..etc. The next step is **"bail"** for the accused – the magistrate or judge decides; If the accused is a flight risk, the bail will be high; Or the accused may be remanded to jail; If not a flight risk, released on his or her own recognizance; If it is a minor offense and the accused pleads guilty, a sentence may be pronounced on the spot; In more serious offenses, the magistrate determines whether a **"Preliminary Hearing"** or **"Grand Jury Process"** is in order. Grand Jury is usually on a federal level or special cases. At the **"Preliminary Hearing"** it is determined whether there is enough evidence that warrants a formal trial. If there is a Grand Jury involved it pretty much determines the same thing as the preliminary hearing. At this point the prosecution presents his or her case of why the accused should be bound over for a formal trial; if it is determined that there is probable cause for a formal trial then the prosecution must file a **"Bill of Information"** with the court where the trial will be held; the Bill of Information consists of the charges against the accused.

The next step is the **"Arraignment"**. At this point the accused is brought in front of the judge in the court where the trial is to take place to respond to the prosecutor's Bill of Information or respond to the Grand Jury indictment. The charges are read by the Clerk of the Court; again, the accused is informed of his or her rights; i.e., the right to be represented by an attorney. At this stage the accused has the following options on pleading; not guilty,   guilty, not guilty by reason of insanity, or   Nolo Contendere (no contest), this means he or she does not deny the facts but yet does not plead guilty of the crime, or the accused claims he or she does not understand the charges. In cases such as the above, the judge could only accept the plea or reject it.   If the accused pleads not guilty, a trial is then set by the judge. If the accused pleads guilty, the judge will sometimes pronounce a sentence immediately; if a guilty plea is accepted, then there is the possibility of a plea bargaining.

The "Plea Bargaining" process is usually done between the prosecutor and the defendant's attorney. The role of the judge in plea bargaining is to make sure that the process was done within the limits of the legal system. Plea bargaining can result in a reduction of charges for the defendant, avoid a conviction record and avoid a felony record. "Deletion of tangent charges" which means dropping other charges pending against the accused, i.e., not to prosecute "vertically", an agreement to dismiss "horizontal" charges. (For this to happen the prosecutor must file what they call a "nolle prosequi" which means "I refuse to prosecute". A repeater charge is dropped from the indictment. This usually applies to repeat offenders.   Another form of plea bargaining is when the defendant pleads guilty in hopes of asking the prosecutor to ask the judge for a lighter sentence, this is called "Sentence Bargaining". If the accused pleads not guilty, then the judge sets a trial date. In preparation for the trial any evidence gathered is shared between the prosecutor and the defense attorney. This evidence is obtained through "Discovery" by the taking of depositions, interrogatories and subpoenas.

"The Criminal Trial" This begins the "Adversarial Process". The adversarial process is when the prosecutor and the defense attorney must present the case in court in the presence of a judge and a jury of the defendant's peers. However before this happens a jury must be selected. "Jury Selection". Jurors are selected from a Jury Pool, which is called "Venire." In some trials there can be between 6 and 12 jurors, depending on the seriousness of the trial. It varies from state to state. However, in criminal cases there are usually 12 jurors. There is a process called "Voir Rule", which is the process of selection of jurors for "cause" or "peremptory challenges". This process is utilized to eliminate any jurors who may know the defendant or someone in his or her family, persons who may have preconceived feelings about the case. The prosecutor may eliminate jurors who may be sympathetic toward the defendant. Once the jury is selected, the next step is the actual trial.

The next step in the process is the "Opening Statements." At this time the Prosecutor and Defense Attorney addresses the jury in regards to how they plan on proving guilt or innocence of the defendant. Note that the burden of proof lies with the prosecutor to prove beyond a reasonable doubt that the defendant is guilty. The prosecutor presents his or her case first by presenting evidence and witnesses. There are two types of evidence that the prosecutor can present and that is "direct" and "circumstantial evidence." Direct evidence speaks for itself, i.e. weapon or eye witness or a confession. Circumstantial evidence suggests a fact by implication or inference, i.e., hearsay evidence. After each witness the defense attorney has the option of cross examining the witnesses. The defense attorney can only ask questions relating to what the prosecutor asked in direct questioning.

After the prosecutor has introduced all his witnesses he or she believes that they have proved beyond a shadow of doubt he or she rests the case. The defense attorney presents his or her case. The defense presents witnesses and the prosecutor has the option to cross examine each witness. After the defense has introduced all witnesses and believes that he has proven the innocence of the defendant, he or she then rests his case. It now time for the Closing Arguments, the prosecution goes first then the defense gives his her Closing Argument. Once this is completed the next   step is instructions to the jury by the judge. The judge then instructs the jury on what they should be deliberating on, i.e., just the facts presented, etc.

"Deliberation" The jury then retires to the jury room to deliberate. The first thing they must do is make a decision of who will be the jury foreman. Once a decision is made the foreman will give a note to the bailiff to give to the judge. The jury returns to the courtroom and either the Clerk of Court usually reads the verdict, while the defendant is standing. Once the verdict is read the judge will set a sentencing date.

The next step is "Sentencing" However before the judge announces sentencing a "Presentence Investigation Report" is conducted for the judge. This report is designed to assist the judge in making his determination of sentencing the defendant. If the defendant is a third time offender, then this would go against him or her. If the judge finds that the defendant has never been in trouble before perhaps the defendant may get a lighter sentence or even perhaps probation depending on the crime. In addition the judge considers mitigating factors or any other circumstances that would help the judge in his decision.

The defendant will either be incarcerated, suspended sentence, probation or reduced sentence, depending on the seriousness of the crime. The "<u>Appeal</u>." Defendants who are convicted can appeal their cases to the Appellate Division of Superior Court. The defendants can file motions to request lighter sentencing or for a new trial but it would have to be in a situation where the defendant's rights were violated during trial in presenting evidence on the part of his attorney or the prosecutor. Or if the judge gave the incorrect instructions to the jurors, etc.

_____

_____

_____

_____

_____

_____

_____

_____

_____

_____

CHAPTER THIRTY-FOUR

PRESIDENTIAL APPOINTMENT ANALYSIS

This is an analysis of former President Bush's presidential judicial appointments. In order to determine the reason for the former President's choices we must examine his political agenda. First the former President wanted to "advance his political agenda at the expense of legal principles", as stated by Alliance For Justice. (2008). Former President Bush wanted to leave his mark on the justice system well after he left office. Before he left office he had appointed thirty-seven (37%) of judges/justices to various levels of the judicial system. (Alliance for Justice 2008).

POLITICAL AGENDA

As far as his political agenda is concerned, "the former President had little respect for the citizens of the United States." (2008). According to Alliance For Justice, his selection of appointees had "a significant and detrimental effect" on issues concerning economically deprived citizens. Consider for example the "right to privacy", approval of the "pay discrimination policy" and his support of "insulation of large corporations from liability for harm caused to Americans." Bush and his appointees were against "communities using the democratic process to ensure racially diverse schools." (Alliance for Justice 2008).

Most importantly, he didn't listen or seek advice from the Senators, as reported by Alliance for Justice. (2008). Bush wanted to be in control. Most of Bush's appointees had similar ideologies. Supreme Court judges are in their positions for life and most other judges/justices are in for at least eight years or more, so the former President knew that his political agenda would be intact for years to come at least until democrats became a majority in the Senate, the House and the Bench. This was definitely his reasoning in his selection process. Bush was and is an ultraconservative republican and for the most part he made sure that his appointees were also. (Biskupic 2008).

THE PURPOSE OF APPOINTMENTS

Understand, "The circuit courts play a substantial role in shaping the law". (Alliance for Justice 2008). Bush appointed ultraconservatives, such as Brett Kavanaugh on the D.C. Circuit, Michael McConnell on the Tenth Circuit and Jeffrey Sutton on the Sixth Circuit - all of which had the same ideologies as the former President. (Alliance for Justice - 2008). Bush also appointed both John Roberts (53) and Samuel Alito (57) to the U.S. Supreme Court. In addition, he appointed Janice Rogers Brown, 58 who was referred to as an "opponent of affirmative action". (Biskupic 2008).

In concluding, the former President wanted to lead this country in the direction of the way of ultraconservative thinking and the only way to achieve this goal he had to place influential ultraconservative thinkers and decision makers in important positions - that being the judicial system. Judges/Justices have the power to change or make laws which were in favor of his ideologies. By doing so it would solidify his political agenda for years to come. (Biskupic 2008).

In summarizing the State of Pennsylvania we will discuss the qualifications and selection process for judges. It will include the method of selection and a description of the method utilized. It will further indicate the removal of judges/justices from the bench. It will also research the State of New Jersey summarizing the method of selection and a description of method utilized in the selection process, as well as the qualifications of judges/justices and the removal process.

That being said, in the Commonwealth of Pennsylvania the Pennsylvania Judiciary is comprised of the Supreme Court (7), the Superior Court (15), the Commonwealth Court (9), the Common Pleas Court (439) and various other courts. Pennsylvania judges are chosen in partisan elections. A partisan election is one where the candidates are listed on the ballot along with a label designating which political party they are affiliated with. The partisan election is also known as the primary elections. Pennsylvania is one of two states that conduct its judicial election in off years in conjunction with municipal elections.

MERIT SELECTION

In an effort to restore the public's trust Governor Rendell attempted in 2007 to implement a "merit selection of judges in a six-pronged proposal". A selection process that will utilize a screening and evaluating process by a "citizen nominating committee", confirmation by the Senate and retention process in which the public would have a nonpartisan vote. It is still not implemented as yet. (America Judicature Society "AJS").

METHOD OF SELECTION PROCESS AND DESCRIPTION

The above being noted, the method of selection and description of the process for Pennsylvania Supreme Court judges/justices consists of partisan elections, Superior Court is also partisan elections, Commonwealth is partisan election and the Court of Common Pleas is as well. The length of term for Supreme Court is ten years, Superior Court is ten years, the Commonwealth Court is ten years and the Court of Common Pleas is as well.

ADDITIONAL TERM

Once a judge has served on the bench for his or her term he or she can elect to serve for an additional term of ten years for each of the above judgeships through a retention election. In a case where there is a vacancy, which is referred to as "Method of Filling Interim Vacancies." (AJS). The judges mentioned earlier are appointed by what is referred to as, "Gubernatorial Appointment with two thirds Senate approval". (AJS).

INTERIM TERM

Going forward, once the Senate has approved the appointment for the interim judges the appointee must be elected in the "next municipal election more than 10 months after vacancy occurs or upon expiration of term". (AJS). This procedure applies to Supreme Court Judges, Superior Court Judges, Commonwealth and Court of Common Pleas Judges, as well.

SELECTION PROCESS FOR CHIEF JUDGE/JUSTICE

The selection process for the Chief Judge/Justice, i.e., Supreme Court Judge/Justice is determined by seniority, the Superior and Commonwealth Court is determined by "peer vote." Lastly, Court of Common Pleas is determined by either "seniority or peer vote". (AJS). The Supreme Court Judge/Justice serves for duration of term, which would be ten years. The other three courts, Superior, Commonwealth and Court of Common Pleas serve for a term of five years.

QUALIFICATIONS

In the Commonwealth of Pennsylvania the qualifications for the Supreme and Superior Court Judge/Justice must have "1 year state resident, maximum age of 70, state bar member." For both Commonwealth Court and the Court of Common Pleas the judge must have, "1 year district resident; maximum age of 70, state bar member." (AJS).

REMOVAL OF JUDGES

There are two methods in which Pennsylvania Judges can be removed from the bench, 1) investigation by the "judicial conduct board" for complaints initiated by individuals or the board itself for judicial misconduct. 2) Or, impeachment by the House of Representatives. The judge must be convicted by "two thirds of the Senate," in order for this to happen. (AJS). Additional information relating to the qualifications, selection process and the removal of judges in the State of Pennsylvania can be found in the Pennsylvania Constitution, Article V, §§ 12, 13 & 14. Section 12 discusses "qualification of justices, judges and justice of peace", while § 13 discusses the "election of justices, judges and justices of the peace" and § 14 discusses the "judicial qualification commission" and § 18 discusses "suspension, removal, discipline and compulsory retirement of judges/justices". (BallotPedia).

NEW JERSEY

In the State of New Jersey the judicial system comprises the Supreme Court (7), Appellate Division-Superior Court (34) and Superior Court (371). The method of selection for the Supreme Court is by "Gubernatorial appointment with senate confirmation." It is the same for superior Court. The Supreme Court Judge/Justice serves for a term of seven years, whereas the Superior Court Judge/Justice serves the same and is "designated by chief justice." The Appellate Division-Superior Court Judge/Justice serves an "indefinite term." (NJ Constitution).

QUALIFICATIONS

The Supreme Court Judge/Justice must have been "admitted to state practice for 10 years." And there is a mandatory retirement age of 70, as like in the State of Pennsylvania. The Superior Court qualifications are the same as the Supreme Court Judge/Justice. When it is time for the selection of a Chief Judge/Justice for the Supreme Court, it is achieved by a gubernatorial appointment with Senate confirmation. For the Superior Court it is designated by the Chief Justice.

INTERIM VACANCIES

Interim vacancies are filled by gubernatorial reappointment with Senate confirmation and they serve for seven years, if appointed. The selection process for reappointment is as follows in the State of New Jersey; 1) attorneys evaluate judges to whom they have participated in their courts; 2) appellate judges evaluate trial court judges when their rulings have been appealed, and 3) the evaluations are shared with the evaluated judge, the assignment judge, the Supreme Court, the Governor, the Senate Judiciary Committee and the Judicial Evaluation Commission.

The above make up what the State of New Jersey calls the "the Judicial Performance Committee," which is headed by a committee chair selected by the Supreme Court. The committee members serve for a three year term. This program is designed to enhance the process of reappointing judges.

REMOVAL OF JUDGES

If, at any time, the justices of the Supreme Court and the judges of the Superior Court is subject to impeachment he or she cannot continue to perform his or her duties until he or she has been acquitted. Judges or Justices can also be subject to removal from office by the Supreme Court. In addition, if any Justice of the Supreme Court or Judge of the Superior Court shows signs of incapacitation, preventing him or her from performing his or her duties, "the Governor shall appoint a commission of three persons," to investigate the allegation, ultimately if found unable to perform his or her judicial duties, they will be subject to removal from the bench.

In concluding this summary, I find that the States of Pennsylvania and New Jersey are similar with regard to its judicial process, as well as, the qualifications for appointing judges. As far as removal of judges/justices from the bench the criteria is definitely the same for misconduct or incapacitation.

DESCRIPTION OF LAW

The Criminal Resource Manual 940 18 U.S.C. Section 1341 – Elements of Mail Fraud states that, "There are two elements in mail fraud: (1) having devised or intending to devise a scheme to defraud (or to perform specified fraudulent acts), and (2) to use the mail for the purpose of executing, or attempting to execute, the scheme specified fraudulent acts)."

RULE OF LAW

It is a federal crime to knowingly and willfully devise and carryout a scheme to defraud, or obtain money or property by false pretenses from individuals by using the United States Mail, yet individuals knowingly violate this law every day. It is difficult to prosecute mail fraud cases unless a victim(s) come forth and report the crime.

In order to be convicted of mail fraud one would have to be found guilty of "purposefully creating a plan to defraud an individual or institution, display intent to commit fraud, mail something – for the purpose of carrying out a fraudulent scheme – through the USPS or private carrier." (See 18 U.S.C. § 1341).

If convicted of mail fraud, which is a felony, it "carries a sentence of up to five years in prison and/or fines of up to $250,000 when individuals are involved and up to 30 years in prison and/or $1,000,000 in fines when a financial institution is involved. (See 18 U.S.C. § 1341).

According to an article printed on the Lawyer Shop website, "an Arizona man was convicted of mail fraud and sentenced to five years of supervised probation, nine months of home detention, and $1 million in victim restitution after executing the age-old envelope-stuffing scam." (Lawyer Shop Website).

"The man ran ads in national magazines, promising to send stuffing materials to everyone who mailed money for supply costs ($18 to $36) to his fictitious company. He mailed instructions on how to run an envelope-stuffing business but no actual materials," as stated in the article. (Lawyer Shop Website).

This type of crime is considered to be a white collar crime. There are so many of these type of violations in magazines on newsstands throughout the United States and other countries.

The Lawyer Shop cited another case about how prosecutors, "proved in 2002 that a Texas man sold roughly $6.5 million in fraudulent certificates of deposit (CDs) via the U.S. Mail to close to 80 investors – most of whom were senior citizens." (Lawyer Shop Website).

The article goes on to say that "the man, who never purchased the CDs, used portions of the money to pay earlier investors and used the rest for personal expenses. More than 45 investors are still owed a total of $3.5 million." (Lawyer Shop Website).

Individuals who are committing mail fraud and is not prosecuted in a timely fashion run the risk of these individuals not being punished for the felony because the law states that, "The statute of limitations for mail fraud and wire fraud prosecutions is five years (18 U.S.C. § 3282), except for mail and wire fraud schemes that affect a financial institution, in which case the statute is ten years (18 U.S.C. § 3293)".

If you think that you are the victim of mail fraud you may report it to the United States Postal Inspection Service by completing an online form that you may retrieve from the Postal Inspectors website.

_____

_____

_____

_____

_____

_____

_____

SECTION V

EVIDENCE-BASED POLICING

CHAPTER THIRTY-FIVE

EVIDENCE BASE POLICING

Evidence-Based Policing (EBP) is designed to research and evaluate daily procedures of police officers and executives. Constantly designing and setting guidelines for improvements of those procedures for the smooth operation of police activities and to assist in better decision making for all personnel.

Evidence-Based Policing:

According to an article written by Lawrence W. Sherman, professor and chair of the Department of Criminology and Criminal Justice at the University of Maryland at College Park, "The new Paradigm of "evidence-based medicine" holds important implications for policing. It suggests that just doing research is not enough and that proactive efforts are required to push accumulated research evidence into practice through national and community guidelines." Sherman infers that the same model used for evidence-based medicine can be used in other areas of society.

An excellent example where evidence-based policing would be instrumental is in incidents such as police brutality. This could lead to evidence-based guidelines by researching the affects police brutality has on the victims, the police, the families of the police and society.

The malicious beating of Rodney Glen King in California on March 3, 1991 sparked outrage among citizens.[1] (See Endnote for brief a summary). This is a perfect example of the need for evidence-based policing. The situation was evaluated and the police officers were tried for the incident. "Four LAPD officers were later tried in a state court for the beating but were acquitted. The announcement of the acquittals sparked the 1992 Los Angeles riots. Later a federal trial for civil rights violations ended with two of the officers found guilty and sent to prison and the other two officers acquitted". As a result of the evidence researched and collected we could infer that the case should have been resolved relatively quickly. Did these officers use good judgment? You could infer that the abuse of authority played a significant role in the entire case from start to finish. I also believe that this case shows both the advantages and disadvantages of evidence-based policing at its best. Yes, EBP will eventually play a significant role in decreasing incidents as referenced above.

Moreover, as procedures are evaluated more closely, there will be a decrease in the amount of lawsuits against law enforcement agencies, such as in wrongful death cases.[2] (See Endnotes for a brief summary). A decision was made. A life was taken. Why? The police officer made a wrong decision. According to the above article the officers had numerous violations. Why? Was it because of the victim's race? Discriminatory practices and over generalization among officers and executives can play a vital role in evidence-based policing. Hopefully, EBP will research and evaluate this particular behavior among law enforcement. It will certainly help to decrease the amount of police brutality and lawsuits.

The collecting of scientific evidence in order to improve the system is positive, however can we really rely on the outcome? How do we know that the research is accurate? In an effort to get guns off the street, Philadelphia promotes, 'Goods for Guns' campaign. According to an article published in the Philadelphia Tribune, March 5, 1999, "Goods for Guns removed 850 weapons off the street." "Semi-automatic pistols, sawed off shotguns, engraved Old West revolvers and rusted hunting rifles – all with the potential to take a life – sat on a table before Philadelphia's top law enforcement officials and anti-violence advocates." This promotion has its advantages and disadvantages. (1) It gets firearms off the street; (2) it is an economic incentive; and (3) it could turn out to be a disadvantage. Why, because the person turning in the guns can purchase a better gun.

Yes, I am sure that the above cases were researched and evaluated to improve the decision making of police and executives as a result of those cases. Hopefully, the policy makers have designed programs to at least decrease the number of police brutality cases in the future. Additionally, the evaluation of those cases can be utilized as models to teach police officers how to better control situations. I believe that evidence-based policing is improving and understandably will improve law enforcement so that society can continue to have faith in the system.

1   "Rodney Glen King was the victim of police brutality committed by the Los Angeles police officers. A bystander, George Holliday, videotaped much of the incident from a distance. The footage showed LAPD officers repeatedly striking King with their batons. A portion of this footage was aired by news agencies around the world, causing public outrage that raised tensions between the black community and the LAPD and increased anger over police brutality and social inequalities in the black community and the worldwide community as a whole."

2   "The off-duty police officer who shot and killed an unarmed 21-year old man in November during a street fight will be stripped of his badge, Police Commissioner Charles H. Ramsey announced yesterday." "Frank Tepper, 43, a 16-year veteran of the force, committed "numerous violations" of Police Department procedures when he opened fire on William Panas Jr. in the Port Richmond neighborhood where they both lived, according to an investigation by the department's Internal Affairs Division."

CHAPTER THIRTY-SIX

STAGES OF CRIMINAL TRIAL/CLOSING ARGUMENTS

This paper will be based on the Closing Arguments. Upon the completion of presenting evidence both the prosecutor and defense attorney pretty much gives a summation of what each has presented as evidence and how they have proved beyond a reasonable doubt guilt or innocence, this is what we call "Closing Arguments". Nonetheless, before we can get to closing arguments there is a process used to first get to the Closing Arguments.

TRIAL INITIATION

Under the Sixth Amendment, defendants have the right to a "Speedy Trial" after indictment, if this doesn't happen, this technicality might permit the defendant to not being tried.

JURY SELECTION

Going forward, at this stage in the stages of a criminal trial is the selection of impartial jury. The prosecutor and the defense attorney gets the opportunity to select jurors whom they believe will vote in their favor. The prosecutor would select jurors who he thinks will be sympathetic to what he will attempt to prove. The defense will want to select jurors who are the defendant's peers and who are impartial. This selection process is important because the jurors should not have any prejudices, bias and the jurors should be made up of the defendant's peers.

OPENING STATEMENTS

This stage in the process is an important stage. At this stage, the Prosecutor opens with his or her Opening Statement. The Prosecutors explains to the jury that the defendant is guilty and how he or she intends to prove that fact. Once the Prosecutor is done with his opening statement the Defense Attorney will give his or her opening statement. At this point, the Defense Attorney has a choice of whether to give an opening statement or whether he or she will leave it until the Closing Argument. In most cases the Defense Attorney will give the opening statement by disputing the charges against the defendant and why the Prosecutor he or she believes the Prosecutor is wrong in the charges against his or her client. The defense explains to the jurors and the court how he or she will prove beyond a shadow of doubt that his or client is innocent of the charges

PRESENTATION OF THE EVIDENCE

This stage in the process is crucial. The Prosecutor will call his first witness to the stand to present evidence in his or her case for the State. This may be an eyewitness to the crime. We refer to this as direct evidence because the witness is giving firsthand information to the actual crime. It is important that the Prosecutor have investigated the witness to make sure that he or she is a creditable witness. If there is anything that has not been researched about the witness the Prosecutor risks his or her case.

Once the Prosecutor is finished questioning the witness the Defense Attorney will cross-examine the witness in order to discredit the witness or his or her testimony. This process may take hours or days, depending upon the witnesses of the Prosecutor. Once the Prosecutor is finished calling witnesses, he or she then rests their case. The time has come for the Defense Attorney to present any witnesses that he or she may have to prove his or her case for the defendant. After each witness, the Prosecutor also has a chance to cross-examine the witnesses called on behalf of the defendant. Again, once the Defense Attorney is finished providing witnesses for the defendant he then rest his case.

At this point is when the Judge, either recesses until the next day to give both sides a chance to prepare for the Closing Arguments. At this point in the process, whatever both sides did not present in evidence or if they think that the jurors were not influenced by what the witnesses said this is the last time for either side to persuade the jury of innocence or guilt.

CLOSING ARGUMENT

Usually, again, the Prosecutor gets to persuade the jury with his or her closing argument. The Closing Argument is normally a summation of the Opening Argument and of all the facts presented during the trial, but with how he or she felt that they proved beyond a shadow of doubt the guilt of the defendant.

In the case of the Defense Attorney, he or she has the option to make an emotional plea for the innocence of the client by reiterating the innocence of the client, type of person the client, and the evidence presented during the trial. If it was a murder trial, the defense will point out once again that the defendant did not murder the victim. He will lay the burden on the jury to see that justice is done. He will ask them to consider all the facts presented in the case. The Defense will also attempt to appeal to the juror's emotions and to envision themselves in the defendant's place, to try to experience what he or she is going through.

CLOSING ARGUMENT OF JOHNNIE COCHRAN

The following are excerpts from the Closing Argument of OJ Simpson murder trial, which I believe that Mr. Cochran appealed to the emotional side of the jurors and the character of Mr. Simpson.

"Mr. Cochran: The Defendant, Mr. Orenthal James Simpson, is now afforded an opportunity to argue the case, if you will, but I'm not going to argue with you, ladies and gentlemen. What I'm going to do is to try and discuss the reasonable inferences which I feel ……………….." "Ultimately, it's what you determine to be the facts is what's going to be important, and all of us can live with that. You are empowered to do justice. You are empowered to ensure that this great system of ours works. Listen for a moment, will you, please. One of my favorite people in history is the great Frederick Douglas. He said shortly after the slaves were freed, quote, "In a composite nation like ours as before the law, there should be no rich, no poor, no high, no low, no white, no black, but common country, common citizenship, equal rights and a common destiny." This marvelous statement was made more than 100 years ago. It's an ideal worth striving for and one that we still strive for. We haven't reached this goal yet, but certainly in this great country of ours, we're trying. With a jury such as this, we hope we can do that in this………………………." "I'd like to comment and to compliment Miss Clark and Mr. Darden on what I thought were fine arguments yesterday. I don't agree with much of what they said, but I listened intently, as I hope you'll do with me."

"And together, hopefully these discussions are going to be helpful to you in trying to arrive at a decision in this case where you don't compromise, where you don't do violence to your conscious (sic), but you do the right thing. And you are the ones who are empowered to determine what is the right thing. Let me ask each of you a question. Have you ever in your life been falsely accused of something? Have you ever been falsely accused? Ever had to sit there and take it and watch the proceedings and wait and wait and wait, all the while knowing that you didn't do it?"

THE CRIMINAL JUSTICE SYSTEM

The Criminal Justice system is made up of three divisions, law enforcement, the court system and corrections. Each division plays a significant role in enforcing the law in order to maintain a relatively safe society for its citizens.

Figure 1 (The Arrest by Police) >>>>> Figure 2 (Adjudication, Sentencing - Court) >>>>> Figure 3 (Imprisonment)

LAW ENFORCEMENT

The Police is the first phase in the Criminal Justice System. The police are usually the first responders to a crime or emergency. The primary role of the police is to enforce the law, prevent crimes, protect the rights and freedoms of individuals as well as maintain public order.

Once a crime has been committed the function and role of the police is to arrest the suspect, gather evidence of a crime through investigation and questioning witnesses, if any. In addition, the law enforcement division (police) respond to emergency 911 calls and provide emergency treatment when necessary.

If there is a crime committed, the police are called to the scene of the crime, if there is probable cause for an arrest, the suspect is arrested and he or she is read his or her Miranda rights. It is the role of the police to book the suspect, taking all necessary information, being sure to protect the individual's rights under the U.S. Constitution.   Just because a person has committed a crime does not mean that they don't have rights. This is the reason for the police informing the suspects of his or her Miranda rights. If the police does not respect these rights and the suspect goes to court he or she can get off on a technicality.

CRIMINAL COURTS

Once a criminal reaches the Criminal Courts Division, the primary function of the court is to conduct a fair and impartial trial by providing check and balances, basically overseeing the fairness of the court process during the trial as relating to due processing. Any individual unfortunate enough to be faced with going to court his or her rights under the U.S. Constitution must be protected. The judge also informs the defendant of his or her rights under the Constitution. If it is trial by jury then the jury determines guilt or innocence. Once guilt is determined the judge imposes sentencing. Depending on the serious of the crime this will determine if the criminal will be incarcerated. Once the judge has imposed sentencing, the next step in the Criminal Justice System is incarceration. The prisoner is sent to a correctional institution to serve out his or her sentence.

CORRECTIONAL INSTITUTION

The primary function of the correctional institution is to house prisoners, rehabilitate and protect their rights under the U.S. Constitution. Prisoners have the same rights of other citizens with the exception their freedom has been revoked for the length of their sentence. The correction institution is responsible for carrying out the sentence imposed by the courts and supervising prisoner's behavior while they are in prison. Once offenders have been rehabilitated they are allowed back into society. In essence, all three components of the Criminal Justice Systems must work together in order to protect the human rights of the accused.

When going to court the rights of the accused under the U.S. Constitution must be protected. The judge also informs the defendant of his or her rights under the Constitution. If it is trial by jury then the jury determines guilt or innocence. Once guilt is determined the judge imposes sentencing. Depending on the serious of the crime this will determine if the criminal will be incarcerated. Once the judge has imposed sentencing, the next step in the Criminal Justice System is incarceration. The prisoner is sent to a correctional institution to serve out his or her sentence.

SECTION VI

THE HISTORY OF U.S. PRISONS

Definition of a Prison

"A state or federal confinement facility that has custodial authority over adults sentenced to confinement."

The Penitentiary Era (1790-1825)

• During this Era is when the Walnut Street Jail was converted into a Penitentiary by the Quakers.

• The Quakers believed that this was an opportunity for prisoners to repent for their crimes.

• The Quakers also believed in the rehabilitation and deterrence. This belief is practiced to this day in prisons.

• Before the Walnut Street Jail became a prison, it was used primarily for a holding jail until trial.

• During this era there were other prisons convicted such as the Eastern Penitentiary in Cherry Hill, Pennsylvania and Western Penitentiary in Pittsburgh, Pennsylvania.

WALNUT STREET JAIL (1790)

Early Development of Penal Practices

- The penalty of death was applied to murder;

- Severe physical punishments were used for lesser crimes;

- Sexual offenses were punished by "fogging";

- Someone accused of stealing punished by "mutilation";

- There were other punishments, such as branding, public humiliation, workhouse and exile.

AUBURN STATE PRISON

Auburn, N. Y. — Auburn State Prison.

The Reformatory Era and the Industrial Era (1876-1890)

- The Reformatory Era consisted believed in rehabilitation and The Elmira Reformatory in Elmira. New York was built about this time to house prisoners. During this period, the Pennsylvania System and the Auburn System was in constant conflict. The outgrown of the system came the Reformatory Era. There were two connections leaders by the names of Captain Alexander Maconochie and Sir Walter Crotton, who were instrumental in developing the Reformatory style of imprisonment.

- "Maconochie developed a system of marks through which prisoners could earn enough credits to buy their freedom." Bad behavior removed credits. The credits helped prisoners to received an early release on prison.

- Sir Walter Crotton, head of the Irish Prison System was impressed with the credit system, he soon adopted the idea of early release. "Crotton was convinced that convicts could not be rehabilitated without successful reintegration into the community."

- The industrial era was based on a correctional model intended to capitalized on the labor of convicts sentenced to confinement. The private sector paid to utilize prisoners as cheap labor. The prisoners made goods made by prisoners under the supervision of the private sector. The prisoners were escorted to the worksites under the supervision or armed guards. The prisoners who worked on the roads or highways, cleaned public parks and recreational facilities, as well as maintained public buildings.

- In 1935, the Ashurts Summers Act, which was passed to prohibit the interstate transportation and sale of prison goods where state laws forbade them. The Ashurts Summers Act, "Federal Legislature of 1935 that effectively ended the industrial prison era by restricting interstate commerce in prison state goods . Basically, all prisoners make today is license plates and anything that would be used for state use only.

The Punitive Era, The Treatment Era and The Community Based Era

- The Punitive Era (1935-2945)
    - o The Punitive Era believed in retribution. The truly dangerous criminals, such as Al Capone and other mob bosses were sent to Alcatraz for their prison sentence.

- The Treatment Era (1945-1967)
    - o The treatment Era focused on the medical treatment of the prisoners and rehabilitation. The officials felt that criminal behavior was the cause of some medical abnormality and had to be treated.

- The Community Based Era (1967-1980)
    - o The Community Based Era focused on "the realities of prison overcrowding combined with a renewed faith in humanity and the treatment ear's belief in the possibility of behavioral change to inspire a movement away from institutionalized corrections and toward the creation of the opportunities for reformation within local communities.

The Warehousing Era and The Just Deserts Era

- The Warehousing Era (1980-1995)
    - o The Warehousing Era is based on "An imprisonment strategy that is based on the desire to prevent recurrent crime and has abandoned all hope of rehabilitation. This era was concerned about protecting society from these dangerous criminals. The purpose was to deter criminals from repeat offenses and to decrease crime. However, the population in prisons grew dramatically during the Warehousing Era as a result of changes sentencing laws primarily taking drug dealers off the streets.

- The Just Deserts Era (1995-Present)
  - o "Warehousing and prison overcrowding were primarily the result of both public and official frustration with rehabilitative efforts." At the end of the Warehousing Era, a new philosophy was introduced, which was the justice model. The emphasis is on individual responsibility. Its focus is on the theory "Just Deserts". "A model of criminal sentencing that holds that criminal offenders deserve the punishment they receive at the hands of the law and that punishments should be appropriate to the type and severity of the crime committed."

PRISON TRENDS IN THE UNITED STATES

Prisons Today

- There are approximately 1,325 stated prisons.
- There are approximately 84 federal prisons across the country.
- The American prison system has more than quadrupled since 1980.
- On January 01, 2007, state and federal prisons held approximately 1,570,861 prisoners. Seven percent of those were women.
- Most individuals sentenced to prisons are convicted of violent crimes.
- Between 1991-2006, the official rate of crime in the U.S. dropped from 5,897 to 3,835 offenses per every 100,000 residents.
- The Few Charitable Trust released a report predicting that the nation's prison population will rise to more that 1.72 million by 2011.

ANALYTICAL REVIEW OF THE CRIMINAL JUSTICE SYSTEM

In our present Criminal Justice System there are challenges within all three components of the system, i.e., law enforcement, court system and corrections. And we cannot analyze one and not the others. Changes must be made on all levels of the criminal justice system. We must first start with law enforcement and what part law enforcement play in society today, especially in lowering overcrowding in our correctional institutions. In order to analyze the system we must ask what are some of the problems? In the court system there are too many juveniles getting to that stage in the system. Why, you may ask? In corrections there are too many juveniles in our correctional institutions. Again, why? The first stage of the system is law enforcement and this is where it all begins. Why, you ask? The challenges law enforcement faces, specifically the arrest of first time juvenile offenders are vast. "For young offenders, law enforcement is often the entry point into the juvenile justice system. When a juvenile is apprehended for the first time for violating the law, it is the police officer who determines the nature of the offender's initial involvement with the justice system", as reported in the Juvenile Offenders and Victims: National Report Series Bulletin.

As mentioned previously the criminal justice system involves three different components, one being the first time a juvenile offenders encounter with law enforcement. Once a crime has been committed it is at this stage law enforcement can make a difference, especially if a law enforcement officer is dealing with a first time juvenile offender. Our correctional institutions are overcrowded partly because of the rise in juvenile offenders. In 1999, juvenile offenders accounted for 16% arrests in violent crime and 32% in property crime. (See National Report Series: Law Enforcement and Juvenile Crime written by Howard N. Snyder, Dec. 2001). "The way law enforcement agencies handle first-time juvenile offenders can affect the juvenile and his or her inclination to continue to violate the law", as reported by "The Police Chief Magazine" article "Reducing Crime through Juvenile Delinquency Intervention, dated February 2010.

There is a need to look at alternative solutions in keeping juveniles out of the criminal justice system. This in itself is a challenge. Reducing crime through juvenile delinquency intervention is a good place to start for law enforcement.

There are challenges facing first time police officers who are anxious to meet their quota with arrests. New police officers are not experienced enough, or have the understanding of the importance of saving a juvenile offender's life, especially if this is a first time offense. "When examining the potential long-term negative impact on the community, the first-time arrest of a juvenile offender is a big arrest that criminal justice professionals cannot afford to treat as trivial," as stated in the Police Chief Magazine. (Page 1, ¶ 1)

At this stage it is important how law enforcement handles a juvenile offender; the situation could have a devastating effect on the juvenile's life. "When handled proactively and with the appropriate gravity, that first police encounter can be a foundational life experience capable of reversing a juvenile offender's downward slide into potentially chronic, serious, and violently delinquency, as well as a key opportunity to achieve significant, long-term crime reductions for the community," as explained in The Police Chief Magazine (Page 2, ¶ 2).

In December 1999, Chicago introduced the Juvenile Intervention Project, which was the first of its kind in Chicago and it made a major difference in reducing juvenile crime. According to the Police Chief Magazine it "makes a major turning point that builds upon the juvenile Gang Intervention Partnership Program (JGIPP), which was first introduced by the Chicago Police Department. (Page 2, ¶1)

Law enforcement plays a vital role in the lives of juvenile offenders because they can determine if the crime is serious enough to warrant whether it continues to the next stage in the criminal justice system. If law enforcement accepts the responsibility of intervention at this stage, as like the Chicago Police Department, juvenile crimes rates will begin to decrease instead of increasing.

There should be a program initiated similar to the one in Chicago in as many states as possible, in an effort to change how law enforcement officers evaluate each individual juvenile offender, i.e., the ages, prior arrests, family background, abuse, etc. If each individual case is evaluated for the above at the beginning of what could become a continuing pattern of criminal behavior perhaps intervention services will be productive and possibly reduce the crime among juvenile offenders.

"Research has shown that intervention efforts with juvenile offenders are more likely to be effective in reducing recidivism when those interventions are attempted at the time of their first few arrests." (http://policechiefmagazine.org

Intervention at an early age should enlighten law enforcement of some of the problems associated with first and second time juvenile offenders are faced with. The Chicago base program have profiled first and second time offenders and found that they are plagued with the following problems, i.e., abuse, neglect, running away, lack of parental supervision; failing in school, suspension, drug or alcohol abuse and gang involvement.

As a result of the research, "Under the project, social workers have been assigned as case managers and perform three particularly key functions with respect to those juvenile offenders diverted from court and identified for intervention services by the youth investigator." The case workers responsibility is to help youth investigators communicate, to both the juveniles and their parents, the seriousness of the situation and the value of social services. Secondly, individualized service plans for each offender is assigned to case management. Lastly, there are regular monitoring and follow-up, which is very important in situations such as this.

As a result of these efforts, the pattern of delinquency will contribute to long-term crime prevention by reducing the number of emerging career criminals, hence lowering overcrowding in the correctional institutions.

Another organization we might want to look at in regards to reducing juveniles from entering the criminal justice system is the Police Athletic League (PAL). At one point PAL was in the news quite a bit; you don't hear too much about PAL today. However, I did managed to get information from the internet regarding the New York City Police Athletic League. "PAL was founded in 1914 by Captain John Sweeney, Commanding Officer of a Lower East Side police precinct. It seems PAL focuses more on prevention rather than intervention. "PAL's mission remains unchanged – to keep young people out of trouble by channeling their energies into recreational and athletic programs.

In 1929 an advisory committee on crime prevention was appointed by Police Commissioner Grover A. Whalen in an effort to address the growing concerns about juvenile delinquency. "It was believed that the trouble-making boy of today would become the hardened criminal of tomorrow." "In an effort to prevent future crime, the Police Department began to focus on the youth of the city, and took a leadership role in providing positive recreation." (Page 2, Crime Prevention Bureau, ¶4) ." For additional information go to (http://www.palnyc.org).

In essence, early intervention at the law enforcement level is seriously needed in an effort to prevent future crime of first and second-time juvenile offenders resulting in the decreasing of overcrowding in the correctional institutions. The need for seriously active participation of law enforcement should definitely be mandatory at all levels.

CRIME IN PERSPECTIVE

Crime is the result of many problems confronting society today, such as economically deprived multicultural groups of people unable to meet their basic needs. Individuals who are unable to maintain a functional household may believe that the only means for survival is to commit an unlawful act in order to provide food and shelter for their families. This is found in some underprivileged groups of people. According to an article from an internet resource states that, "The type of crime traditionally associated with economic inequality is property crime. In recent years, however, the "deep anger" explanation has become more popular, and many criminologists now associate economic inequality with violent crime. Perhaps the most common association is with "conventional" or street crime. For example, when unemployment goes up 1%, there's a 4% increase in homicides, a 6% increase in robberies, a 2% increase in burglaries, and measurable effects on rape and other crimes." (Internet Resource: Poverty, Inequality, and Grime. www.apsu.edu/oconnort/crim/crimtheory09.htm)

In addition, crime is also the result of one of the oldest culprits, simple greed. Greed is a powerful motivator for committing an unlawful act. For example, let us examine the case of the Menendez brothers who killed their parents on August 20, 1989 for $14 million dollars. As referenced by internet resources, "The Menendez murder spending spree-including a Porsche and two restaurants-helped convince a jury that their motivation was just plain greed." (Internet Resources – Newsweek – "When Wealthy Children Grow up to be Bad People").

CHAPTER THIRTY-SEVEN

M. HOLMES' VIEW

Who am I, Who are you and What can you do?

Who am I? I am a seventy-three year old great grandmother who is still employed every day because I cannot afford to retire. I still have a mortgage to pay and a household to sustain. I would be on the street if I did not work. Social security cannot sustain the lifestyle that I am accustomed to. Don't get me wrong I still enjoy working, but I cannot retire just yet. At this juncture in my life I want to live in peace, take care of my pets and maintain my place of residence. Did I not tell you, I also enjoy writing? In addition, I hold two degrees, one in journalism and the other in criminal justice. I have raised a son on my own, who passed away in 2017. I still miss him tremendously, but I know that he would not want me to be depressed, so I continue to go on every day. I miss him every day, but he left me with two granddaughters and a great grandson. I thank God for them.

This book covers many topics because these are the topics that I am most concerned about. The book is not in any particular order but I believe that everyone who reads this book will find something of interest that they will be passionate about. I hope that I can reach at least one of you, if not many of you, to just take a stand and do something to make this world a better place. Just, start in your community where it all begins. Once you realize that the community where you live, within each home is where you begin to make positive changes.

THE END

BIBLIOGRAPHY

1. Internet Resources: Poverty, Inequality, and Grime: www.apsu.edu/oconnort/crim/crimtheory09.htm

2. Internet Resources: Newsweek "When Wealthy Children Grow up to be Bad People" http://photo.newsweek.com/2010/1/rotten-rich-kids.slide7.html
   28 .S. C.A. § 534.

3. James B. Jacobs and Kimberly A. Potter, "Hate Crimes" A Critical Perspective," in Michael Tonry, ed., Crime and Justice: A Review of Research (Chicago: University of Chicago Press, 1997), p.19

4. Bureau of Justice Assistance, Addressing Hate Crimes: Six Initiatives That Are Enhancing the Efforts of Criminal Justice Practitioners (Washington, DC: U.S. Department of Justice, 2000).

5. Criminology Toda, an Integrative Introduction, Fifth Edition, Frank Schmalleger, Ph.D.

6. Internet Resources, Crime Index: The FBI's Uniform Crime Reports, Associated Content, http://www.associatedcontent.com

7. Life – http://www.msnbc.com/id/35475336/ns/us_news-life/

8. Newsweek - http://photo.newsweek.com/2010/recent-history-of-anti-tax-violence-in-the-us/tax-attachks.html

9. Internet: Delaware County Daily Times, http://www.delcotimes.com/articles/2010/02/22/news/news/doc4b8203db608a4721289910

10. Article: Update: Brothers get jail time in credit union scam, Published: Monday, February 22, 2010

11. Article: Judge decides to go easy on union executive, published: Tuesday, February 23, 2010

12. Internet: Philadelphia Inquirer, http://www.philly.com/inquirer/breaking/news_breaking/20100222_credit_union_VP..Published February 22, 2010

13. The Prevention and Detection of Business Fraud: The role of Management and the Changing Role of…. Author: B.R. Farrell – 1999 cited by 5 – Related Articles

14. Swinton, L (n.d.). Ethical Decision Making: How to Make Ethical Decision in 5 Steps. Retrieved November 4, 2010, from http://www.mftrou.com

15. Ethics, Crime, and Criminal Justice. (2008). Pearson Prentice Hall. Upper Saddle River, NJ. William C.R. & Arrigo, B.A.

16. Velasquez, M., Andre, C., Shanks, T. S.J. & Meyer, M.J. (Revised 2010). What is Ethics? Markkula Center for Applied Ethics. Retrieved October 23, from http://www.scu.edu/ethics/practicing/decision/whatisethics.html)

17. New World Encyclopedia. Retrieved October 23, from (http://www.newworldencyclopedia.org/entry/normative_ethics)

18. Sweet, W. (Updated, 2008). Internet Encyclopedia. Jeremy Bentham (1748-1832). Retrieved October 23, from (http://www.iep.utm.edu/bentham/).

19. Joseph, J. (2000). Ethics in the Workplace. Retrieved October 23, from Ethics Resource Center, Inc. (http://www.asaecenter.org/Resources/articledetail.cfm?itemnumber=13073).

20. Cavalier, R. (2002). Meta-ethics, Normative Ethics, and Applied Ethics. Retrieved October 18, from Online Guide to Ethics and Moral Philosophy. (http://caae.phil.cmu.edu/cavalier/80130/part2/II_preface.html).

21. Sullivan, O. & Pecorino, P.A. (002). Ethics: Chapter One: Introduction. Section 2. Normative Ethics and Metaethics. Retrieved October 18, from (http://2.sunysuffolk.edu/pecorip/scccweb/etexts/ethics/chapter_1_introduction).

22. Seymour, A. (1998). Organizational Leadership. U.S. Department of Justice. Retrieved December 11, 2010. Retrieved from: http://www.ncjrs.gov

23. Top 10 Qualities of Criminal Justice Professionals. (n.d.). Retrieved December 9, 2010. Retrieved from http://www.criminaljusticedegree.org

24. Vick, A. (Updated August 23, 2010). Personal Code of Ethics in Criminal Justice. Retrieved: December 11, 2010. Retrieved from: http://www.ehow.com

25. Dodson, J. (n.d.). Integrity Centered-Leadership. Dodson Training Resources, Inc. Seminar. Retrieved December 11, 2010. Retrieved from http://www.dodsontraining.com/courses.htm

26. Seymour, A. (1998). Organizational Leadership. U.S. Department of Justice. Retrieved December 11, 2010. Retrieved from: http://www.ncjrs.gov

27. Top 10 Qualities of Criminal Justice Professionals. (n.d.). Retrieved December 9, 2010. Retrieved from http://www.criminaljusticedegree.org

28. Vick, A. (Updated August 23, 2010). Personal Code of Ethics in Criminal Justice. Retrieved: December 11, 2010. Retrieved from: http://www.ehow.com

29. Dodson, J. (n.d.). Integrity Centered-Leadership. Dodson Training Resources, Inc. Seminar. Retrieved December 11, 2010. Retrieved from http://www.dodsontraining.com/courses.htm

30. Crain, W.C. (1985). Theories of Development. Kohlberg's Stages of Moral Development. Retrieved November 16, 2010. Retrieved from http://faculty.plts.edu/gpence/html/kohlberg.htm

31. The MOVE bombing, 1985. (2007). Retrieved November 16, 2010. Retrieved from http://libcom.org/library/move-bombing - 1985

32. Sullivan, L. (2005). Philadelphia MOVE Bombing Still Haunts Survivors. Retrieved on November 21, 2010. Retrieved from http://www.npr.org/templates/story/story.php?storyId=4651126

33. International Encyclopedia of Philosophy. (IEP). Legal Moralism. Retrieved October 30, 2010 from Website address: http://www.iep.vtm.edulaw.phil/#ssh2a.i

34. International Encyclopedia of Philosophy. (IEP). Legal Paternalism. Retrieved October 30, 2010 from Website address: http://www.iep.vtm.edulaw.phil/#ssh2a.i

35. Hart, H.L.A. (1963). Law, Liberty and Morality. Retrieved October 30, 2010 from International Encyclopedia of Philosophy. (IEP). Website address: http://www.iep.vtm.edulaw.phil/#ssh2a.i

36. Dworkin, G. (1972). Retrieved October 30, 2010 from International Encyclopedia of Philosophy. (IEP). Website address: http://www.iep.vtm.edulaw.phil/#ssh2a.i

37. Jones, C. (2010). About Millionaires Who Give Away Money. Retrieved October 30, 2010 from http://www.ehow.com/about_462299_millionaires-who-give-away-money.html

38. Research Website: Juvenile Crime Statistics – On Lawyer Source. Retrieved June 29, 2010 from www.onlinelawyersource.com.

39. Krisberg B. (2005). Reforming Juvenile Justice. Retrieved June 29, 2010 from www.prospect.org.

40. **Miller E. (2010). Juvenile Justice and Delinquency Prevention Act of 1974. Retrieved June 29, 2010   from** www.enotes.com

41. Research Website: Juvenile Justice and Delinquency Prevention Act. Retrieved from www.answers.com.

42. Research Website: Photos: World's Rottenest Rich Kids. (http://photonewsweek.com).

43. Krisberg B. (2005). Reforming Juvenile Justice. (www.prospect.org). Retrieved July 9, 2010.

44. Adams W., Arnold J., Harmon A., Mayabb H, Rodriquez R. & Shirolo A. Cures for Juvenile Delinquency. (home.snu.edu). Retrieved July 9, 2010.

45. Research Website: Juvenile Delinquency – Family Structure – Single Parent, Poverty, Theory and Development. http://famil.jrank.org/pages/a006/juvenile-Delinquency-Family-Sturcture.html. Retrieved July 9, 2010.

46. Munson W. (2010). Recreation and Juvenile Delinquency Prevention: How Recreation Professionals Can Design Programs that Really Work. http://findarticles.com/p/articles/mi_mll45/is_6_37/ai_88702659. Retrieved May 11, 2010.

47. Research Website: Juvenile Delinquency, Chapter 7, World Youth Report (2003), p.190. PDF Document.

48. Morse J. (2003). Parents or Prisons. Policy Review. http://findarticles.com/p/articles/mi_qa3647/is_200308/ai_9255933.

49. Research Website. Center on Juvenile & Criminal Justice. Juvenile Justice System Flowchart. Retrieved from (www.cjcj.org.)

50. Juvenile Justice: Policies, Programs and Practices. (3rd Ed.). New York, NY: Taylor R. W., Fritsch E. J.

51. Juvenile Justice: Policies, Programs, and Practices. (2010). (3rd Ed.). New York, NY: Taylor, R.W., Fritsch, E.J.

52. Research Website: http://www.ncjrs.gov/html/ojjdp). The Office of Juvenile Justice and Delinquency Prevention.

53. Research Website: Photos: World's Rottenest Rich Kids. (http://photonewsweek.com).

54. Krisberg B. (2005). Reforming Juvenile Justice. (www.prospect.org). Retrieved July 9, 2010.

55. Adams W., Arnold J., Harmon A., Mayabb H, Rodriquez R. & Shirolo A. Cures for Juvenile Delinquency. (home.snu.edu). Retrieved July 9, 2010.

56. Research Website: Juvenile Delinquency – Family Structure – Single Parent, Poverty, Theory and Development. http://famil.jrank.org/pages/a006/juvenile-Delinquency-Family-Sturcture.html. Retrieved July 9, 2010.

57. Munson W. (2010). Recreation and Juvenile Delinquency Prevention: How Recreation Professionals Can Design Programs that Really Work. http://findarticles.com/p/articles/mi_mll45/is_6_37/ai_88702659. Retrieved May 11, 2010.

58. Research Website: Juvenile Delinquency, Chapter 7, World Youth Report (2003), p.190. PDF Document.

59. Morse J. (2003). Parents or Prisons. Policy Review. http://findarticles.com/p/articles/mi_qa3647/is_200308/ai_9255933.

60. Research Website: (http://www.homeboy-industries.org/employment-services.php).

61. Rimkus Consulting Group, Inc. (2010). U.S. Supreme Court. Retrieved December 12, 2010, from http://caselaw.lp.findlaw.com/us/347/483-html

62. Judicial Process in America. (2011). 8th Edition. Chapter 12. Pgs. 292-300. Carp, R.A., R. Stidham & K.L. Manning.

63. Group Behavior in Social Psychology. Stephen L. Franzoi . McGraw-Hill Learning Solutions (2009). Custom Edition. (Chapter 8, pgs. 301-303). .

64. Code of Judicial Conduct. Retrieved November 29, 2010. Retrieved from   http://www.lasc.org/rules/supreme/cjc.asp

65. Ehrlich, E., Flexner, S.B., Carruth, G. and Hawkins J.M. (1980). Oxford American Dictionary. New York Oxford. Oxford University Press. Pleasantville, New York. Retrieved on   November 27, 2010.

66. Juvenile Justice: Policies, Programs and Practices. (3rd Ed.). New York, NY: Taylor R. W., Fritsch E. J.

67. Criminal Justice Today, An Introductory Text for the 21st Century. Author: Frank Schmalleger, Tenth Edition.

68. Internet Resources: Pictures

69. American Judicature Society. Judicial Selection Materials. (n.d.).   Retrieved October 30, 2010 from http://www.selection.us/judicial_selection_materials

70. American Judicature Society. Methods of Judicial Selection. (n.d). Retrieved October 30,   2010 from http://www.selection.us/judicial_selection_materials

71. American Judicature Society. Research on Judicial Selection. (n.d). Retrieved October 30, 2010 from   http://www.selection.us/judicial_selection_materials

72. American Judicature Society. Removal of Judges. (n.d.). Retrieved October 30, 2010 from http://www.selection.us/judicial_selection_materials

73. New Jersey State Constitution. (1947). (Updated through amendments adopted in November 2008). Retrieved October 30, 2010 from New Jersey State Constitution. Article VI,   Sections VI, V, (amended effective December 7, 1978).   http:/www.njleg.state.nj.us/lawsconstitution/constitution.asp

74. Research Website: Photos: World's Rottenest Rich Kids. (http://photonewsweek.com).

75. Krisberg B. (2005). Reforming Juvenile Justice. (www.prospect.org). Retrieved July 9, 2010.

76. Adams W., Arnold J., Harmon A., Mayabb H, Rodriquez R. & Shirolo A. Cures for Juvenile Delinquency. (home.snu.edu). Retrieved July 9, 2010.

77. Research Website: Juvenile Delinquency – Family Structure – Single Parent, Poverty, Theory and Development. http://famil.jrank.org/pages/a006/juvenile-Delinquency-Family-Sturcture.html. Retrieved July 9, 2010.

78. Munson W. (2010). Recreation and Juvenile Delinquency Prevention: How Recreation Professionals Can Design Programs that Really Work. http://findarticles.com/p/articles/mi_mll45/is_6_37/ai_88702659. Retrieved May 11, 2010.

79. Research Website: Juvenile Delinquency, Chapter 7, World Youth Report (2003), p.190. PDF Document.

80. Morse J. (2003). Parents or Prisons. Policy Review.   http://findarticles.com/p/articles/mi_qa3647/is_200308/ai_9255933.

81. Conducting Research in Social Psychology. McGraw-Hill Learning Solutions (2009).

82. Custom Edition. (Chapter 2, pgs. 33, 43). Retrieved April 17, 2010.

83. Internet Reference. Correlational Study.

84. Research website: (http://www.psychologyandsociety.com/correlationalstudy.html).   Retrieved April 17, 2010.

85. Cherry, K. (2010). The Purpose of Correlational Studies. (p. 1). Retrieved April 17, 2010, About.com Guide from (www.psychology.about.com)

86. Delaware County Community Service and Training Center. Confidential Interview, Juvenile, Jeremy. (May 2010). (www.co.delaware.pa.us/depts/corrections.html).

87. Retrieved from the Delaware County website. The Department of Community Corrections. (www.co.de.aware.pa.us).

88. Juvenile Justice: Policies, Programs, and Practices. (2010). (3rd Ed.). New York, NY: Taylor, R.W., Fritsch, E.J.

89. Juvenile Justice: Policies, Programs, and Practices. (2010). (3rd Ed.). New York, NY: Taylor,   R.W., Fritsch, E.J.

90. Research Website: (http://www.helium.com). Article: Juvenile Delinquency.

91. Research Website: (http://www.ojjdp.ncjrs.gov/PUBS/drugid/ration-03.html).

92. Article: Consequences of youth substance abuse.

93. Research Website: (www.at-risk.com). Article: The Development of Juvenile Institutionalization.

94. Research Website: (www.resiliency.com). Article: Resiliency and the Cycle of Change.

95. Juvenile Justice: Policies, Programs and Practices. (3rd Ed.). New York, NY: Taylor R. W., Fritsch E. J.

96. Internet Reference. License Plate Camera Systems. Surveillance Video.com. (n.d). (http://www.sur-veillance-video.com/ea-license.html)

97. Internet Reference. Security Camera Systems. Surveillance Video.com. (n.d). (http://www.surveil-lance-video.com/comsys.html)

98. Internet Reference. POD Program. Crime Surveillance Innovations in Chicago. Law Enforcement and Homeland Security Protection. (n.d). (https://portal.chicagopolice.org).

99. Delaware County Community Service and Training Center. Confidential Interview, Juvenile, Jeremy. (May 2010). (www.co.delaware.pa.us/depts/corrections.html).

100.   Munson, W. (2002). Reference Publications. Recreation and juvenile delinquency preven-tion: how recreation professionals can design programs that really work – Research Update. (http://findarticles.com).

101.   Wootton J. & Heck, R. (May 2010).How State and Local Officials Can Combat Violent Juvenile   Crime. (http://www.leaderu.com/socialsciences/juvenile.html).

102.   Internet Reference. POD Program. Police Observation Devices. (n.d). (https://portal.chica-gopolice.org)

103.   Stephen L. Franzoi. Social Psychology (2009) Custom Edition. McGraw-Hill Learning Solutions. Chapter One. p. 8. Introducing Social Psychology.

104.   Kendall, D.T. (2004). The Washington Post. A Big Question about Clarence Thomas. Retrieved October 30, 2010 from http://www.washingtonpost.com/wp-dyn/article/A31117-2004 oct13.htm/

105.   Carp, R. A., Stidham, R. & Manning, K.L. (2011). Judicial Process in America. 8th Edition.   Chapters 9, 10 & 11.

106.   The Criminal Justice process. Retrieved on November 14, 2010. Retrieved from http://www.judiciary.state.nj.us/criminal/crproc.htm

107.   Alliance for Justice. (2008). Judicial Selection during the Bush Administration: 2008 Edition http://www.afj.org.

108.   Biskupic J. USA Today. (2008). Bush's Conservatism to Live Long in the U.S. Retrieved from   http://www.usatoday.com/news/washington/2008-03-13-judges_N.htm

109.   Lawrence W. Sherman, (July, 1998). Evidence-Based Policing. Ideas in American Policing. Retrieved from Internet.

110.   Wikipedia, the free encyclopedia. Retrieved from http://en.wikipedia.org/wiki/ rodney_king.

111.   Allison Steele. Philadelphia officer to be stripped of badge for killing unarmed man.   Philadelphia Inquirer. Retrieved from http://www.philly.com/inquirer/local/20100105_phila_officer

112.   Publisher: Robert Bogle. (March 05, 1999). 'Goods for Guns' removes 850 weapons off the street. Philadelphia Tribune.

113.   Retrieved from http://www.highbeam.com/doc/1p1-23668393.htm1

114.   Carl J. Jensen III, Ph.D. (February 2006). Consuming and Applying Research Evidence-Based Policing.

115.   The Police Chief Magazine. Retrieved from http://policechiefmagazine.org/magazine/index.cfm?fuseaction=display_arch@article_id=815

116.   Internet Reference: http://www.law.umkc.edu/faculty/projects/ftrials/simpson/cochranclose.html

117. The Police Chief Magazine: (February 2010) "Reducing Crime through Juvenile Delinquency Intervention; http://policechiefmagazine.org

118.   History of Police Athletic League NYC: http://palnyc.org

119.   U.S. Department of Justice, Office of Justice Programs, Office of Juvenile Justice and Delinquency Prevention: National Report Series Bulletin, Dec. 2001.

120.   Criminal Justice Today, An Introductory Text for the 21st Century. Author: Frank Schmalleger, Tenth Edition.

Printed in the United States
By Bookmasters